PRIMAL CRAVINGS
YOUR FAVORITE FOODS MADE PALEO

Megan McCullough Keatley and Brandon Keatley

PRIMAL CRAVINGS

This book is intended as a reference volume only, not as a medical manual. The information given here is designed to help you make informed decisions about your health. It is not intended as a substitute for any treatment that may be subscribed by your doctor. If you suspect you have a medical problem, we urge you to seek competent medical help.

Mention of specific companies, organizations, or authorities in this book does not imply endorsement by the author or publisher. Information in this book was accurate at the time researched. The authors received no incentives or compensation to promote the item recommendations in the book.

Library of Congress Control Number: 2013903303

Library of Congress Cataloging-in-Publication Data is on file with the publisher

Keatley, Megan McCullough 1985- ; and Keatley, Brandon, 1983-

Primal Cravings / Megan McCullough Keatley and Brandon Keatley

ISBN: 978-0-9847551-9-6

1. Cooking 2. Health 3. Diet 4. Low carb

Editor: Jessica Taylor Tudzin
Copy Editor: Nancy Wong Bryan
Design and Layout: Megan McCullough Keatley and Caroline De Vita
Cover Design: Janée Meadows
Illustrations: Danna Ray
Photos on page 8, 11, 36, 37 and back cover: Jodi Jones Photography
Food photography: Megan McCullough Keatley

Publisher: Primal Blueprint Publishing. 23805 Stuart Ranch Rd. Suite 145 Malibu, CA 90265

For information on quantity discounts, please call 888-774-6259 or visit PrimalBlueprintPublishing.com

ACKNOWLEDGMENTS AND THANK YOUS

A heartfelt thank you to our families for making us who we are, and for all the great choices you've made in your lives.

Our greatest appreciation to Mark Sisson for being an inspiration and for making this book a reality.

Shout out to our recipe tasters and testers—for your time, taste buds, and feedback.

And last, but not least, we want to thank the readers of our blog, Health-Bent.com. Without your support, comments, and feedback, this book wouldn't have been possible.

DISCLAIMER

CONTENTS

WELCOME

Primal Cravings has been in the making for nearly a decade. It isn't that we've been developing the recipes for that many years; it's because this book ultimately represents our growth as individuals, and as a couple. The influence we've had on each other has shaped what we believe in and how we go about daily life. Good food is our common ground!

But we haven't always defined "good food" in the same way. We met in college at the University of South Carolina in 2004. While pursuing a corporate finance degree, Megan worked as an executive pastry chef in the kitchen of one of South Carolina's top fine-dining bistros, whipping up cakes and tarts, crème brûlées, soufflés, bread puddings, and ice creams. To Megan, food was much more than nutrition. It was an art form. It was a way to express creativity and enjoy every aspect of the process, from kitchen to table. Brandon saw it differently. A student of engineering with a love for all kinds of sports and fitness pursuits, he regarded taste, texture, and savoriness as inconsequential as long as food provided high-quality fuel for the body. As you might imagine, our wildly differing approaches to food led to some serious contention as we began spending more time with each other, and consequently sharing more meals.

Gradually, mutual respect won out. After all, we each had valid points. And so began our foray into planning and cooking meals together, creating cuisine that was as artistic, flavorful, and enjoyable as it was nourishing and life-giving. Eventually the months gave way to years and now here we are, married and cooking meals that we believe are far superior than anything either one of us could have previously imagined back in those early years.

Our opinion on what a healthy lifestyle means has evolved as well. When we first met, we both subscribed to the low-fat, calorie-conscious diet prescribed by conventional wisdom. However, in 2006, we discovered the Primal/paleo lifestyle. After much research and investigation into this seemingly radical new approach, we started to accept the idea of bucking the status quo. But as with anything new and different, we weren't willing to accept everything at face value. We spent years digging deeper, gaining a better understanding and refining what Primal/paleo means to us. As we'll detail in the next section of this book, we distilled our research and created a place to share all that we learned on the web.

When we launched Health-Bent.com, we were out to prove that a diet absent of staples from the standard American diet needn't leave anyone feeling deprived. You might even say we were hell-bent on it! In the years since we started the site, it's grown organically into something we're very proud of, offering healthful alternatives to the foods you thought you couldn't eat. We like to say *Primal Cravings* is "food you want to want to eat." That is, nutrient-dense food that you can really get excited about eating. Sure, grilled chicken over a salad can be tasty. But creating a lifelong passion for healthful eating requires more variety, more soul.

In addition to running Health-Bent, we are both CrossFit coaches, teaching Primal/paleo principles and guiding our clients through their transition to cleaner and more enjoyable eating. The folks we work with on a daily basis confirm that our ideas work in the real world. Based on their feedback and results, they have experienced profound lifestyle changes by using recipes that offer variety and flexibility.

We know our nutrient-dense diet has us feeling and performing better than ever, too. In 2012, we competed together on our affiliate team and placed 7th in the Cross-Fit Games Southeast Regional. When we aren't coaching or training, we enjoy traveling and doing home improvement projects. But most of our time at home is spent learning more about nutrition and cooking, and, of course, creating delicious recipes that have it all. It's who we are.

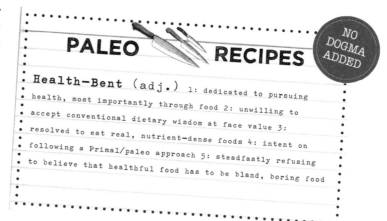

PALEO RECIPES

NO DOGMA ADDED

Health-Bent (adj.) 1: dedicated to pursuing health, most importantly through food 2: unwilling to accept conventional dietary wisdom at face value 3: resolved to eat real, nutrient-dense foods 4: intent on following a Primal/paleo approach 5: steadfastly refusing to believe that healthful food has to be bland, boring food

—Brandon Keatley + Megan Keatley

OUR PHILOSOPHY

We like to eat good food, plain and simple. We also like to feel great and be healthy and productive. We do not believe that these two things have to be mutually exclusive.

Whether they are comforting to us, are associated with fond memories, or stem from curiosity to find variety and seek out new tastes, the desire for flavorful foods is universal. But we also want our food to be nourishing. It's in that spirit that we set out to provide the best of both worlds, with foods that satiate our deep-seated, visceral urges, made from ingredients that satisfy our ancient, genetic needs for good health.

We're talking about outstanding flavors that you may already know and love, often with an interesting—and healthier—twist. It's as simple as omitting the unhealthy ingredients in your favorite foods by changing the vehicle that delivers the flavors. For example, you'll find many of the ingredients and all of the flavor of a Philly cheesesteak sandwich in our Philly Stuffed Peppers recipe. Same thing with the Chicago dog that we've transformed into a kebab. The end result is the best food we've ever made, and we're excited to bring it to your kitchen.

GUIDED BY PRIMAL/PALEO PRINCIPLES

Fun, tasty, and flexible recipes are this book's primary intent. The recipes are guided by principles that also make them healthy choices, so we'd be remiss if we didn't touch on what those principles are and how we use them.

Perhaps you're already familiar with the Primal/paleo movement. Or maybe you are just coming to know about it. For the sake of convenience, we offer the following primer.

The Primal/paleo way of eating is, at its core, about finding the perfect human diet. We look to evolution for answers, adapting a diet informed by the past, thus providing our *homo sapiens* genes the influences they "expect" for optimal health.

The terms Primal and paleo refer to the diets of our primitive ancestors. Research by evolutionary biologists and anthropologists suggest that during the Paleolithic Era, obesity, cardiac disease, diabetes, high blood pressure, and many other diseases either did not exist or were many orders of magnitude less prevalent than they are today. We commonly refer to our Paleolithic ancestors as hunter-gatherers because they had not yet adopted an agrarian (agricultural-farming) lifestyle and obtained their food from, well, hunting and gathering.

Our ancestors were exceptionally fit and healthy by today's standards—they had to be in order to survive! And while their life expectancy was low due to the primitive dangers and health hazards they faced (as well as a complete lack of medical care), those who avoided rudimentary traumas commonly lived six or seven decades in robust health!

Genetically speaking, we are still identical to our Paleolithic ancestors. But unlike them, we are plagued by widespread disease and obesity, despite all our modern information and conveniences. And the problem seems to be getting worse each year, raising the question: What has gone so terribly wrong since Paleolithic times?

When we speak of Primal/paleo, we are essentially talking about informing our diets with the foods from which our species evolved over 2.5 million years. These foods supply all the macro and micro nutrition that the human body needs to thrive. As Mark Sisson reminds us in his book, *The Primal Blueprint*, the principles of Primal/paleo are not new, but "as old as the dawn of mankind, reinforming us about the fundamentals of health that seem to have been forgotten, or misinterpreted, in the modern world."

It's pretty simple stuff, really. But don't let that fool you into thinking there is no variety. When we examine indigenous peoples who live similarly to our ancestors, we see that their diets vary greatly with the climate and geography. That is to say, there is no single ideal diet. For example, some people, such as the traditional Inuit in the Arctic, subsist on a high-fat, high-protein diet, made up mostly from whale, seal, walrus, and caribou. Others, such as the Tukisenta people of Papua New Guinea, thrive almost exclusively on starchy tubers. Yet both groups, as well as many other hunter-gatherer societies throughout the world and throughout history, live or have lived essentially free of disease with naturally lean bodies. Regardless of the variation in diets, the universal characteristics among them all still boil down to two types of food: edible plants and animals.

So, is there more to it than a romantic idea of a time free of cancers, heart disease, diabetes, and the like?

We're glad you asked. Yes, there is a whole lot more. As mentioned, a Primal/paleo diet provides the template for optimal living. It leads us down a path to vibrant health that modern science can substantiate. Though we may think some of the staple foods we consume today—grains, for instance—have been with us a long time, the truth is such foods have been available to us a relatively short time in our 2.5 million-year-old evolutionary history (we're talking .004 percent!), so we haven't evolved any complex adaptations to process them effectively.

Along with anthropology, we also turn to science for answers, asking: What's changed? What's new? What modern foods can we enjoy without evolutionary penalty?

FLAVOR CRAVINGS

Say the food you are making at home is healthy, but, well, kind of boring. Maybe it lacks depth, surprise, or emotion. How much more likely would it be for you to fall prey to all the guilty pleasures out there—the comfort food, the fast food, the packaged junk food—just waiting on your moment of weakness when you get a hankering for something rich, yummy, and soul-satisfying? It's the kind of thing that could have you falling out of love with your healthy lifestyle very quickly. We would not be ashamed to say that we would likely fall face first into something like that ourselves if we had nothing to satisfy us at home.

We call these wanderings off the regimen "flavor cravings." Seeking palatability is a very basic craving we all have, and the ability to enjoy something otherwise utilitarian (fuel/energy/nutrients) really is something that makes us human. Denying ourselves pleasurable food not only goes against our nature, but is unjustly impractical compared to eating mindfully. For that reason we've created healthful alternatives to compete with the unhealthy all-American favorites out there. It's all about staying healthy while enjoying life.

Hippocrates taught us to let food be our medicine, a principle fully embraced by the Primal/paleo community. When we eat the way our ancestors did, we allow our food to return us to good health. In addition to medicine, food acts as information. Once food enters our bodies, our cells are informed about the conditions of the exterior environment, and in reaction to that information, our cells respond accordingly, either activating or deactivating certain genes that will allow us to adapt to the current circumstances. There is nothing in our environment that has no influence on our genes. The sunlight we receive, our activity level, the amount of stressful or relaxing situations we regularly encounter, and yes, even, and most especially, the foods we eat, they all serve as information.

What this means is that while our genetic code (DNA) is fixed and unchanging, the ways our genes are signaled are not. A field of study called *epigenetics* sheds light on how all this works. Essentially, if we think of our genes as computer hardware (our physical computer), then the environment is the computer software (computer programs) that tell our genes what to do. This is known as "gene expression."

A study by the Spanish National Cancer Center illustrated the environmental effects on our genes when it found that the more separate and the more different the lifestyles of identical twins, the less their gene expressions had in common—even though the twins possessed identical DNA! In some twins, one was diagnosed with cancer while the other remained cancer-free.

All of us have strong predispositions coded into our familial genes. Some of us even have a genetic predisposition for obesity, arthritis, or other such maladies. But even genetic bad luck requires a lifestyle component to play out—without that influence, it will likely lie dormant. And in the same way, the genetic recipe for the perfect human being, standing proud after conquering more than two million years of selection pressure resides in each one of us. All you have to do is deliver the proper environmental signals to experience your personal potential, and (no matter how bad your familial genes are) skate right past the health problems caused when genetic predispositions encounter adverse lifestyle practices.

So, the bad news is we can't use our genes as an excuse anymore; the good news is, we can't use our genes as an excuse anymore! Your fate is not predetermined—it's up to you! Without a doubt, the Primal/paleo way of eating promotes optimal gene expression. But this need not be a reenactment of days gone by. You have the flexibility to strike your own balance and work around your personal preferences. It's just a matter of sorting out which of today's foods are beneficial and which are not. Once you do that, technology and progress can work to your benefit instead of your detriment.

To get started, let's build a model that shows the relationship of all of the factors at play. Think of it as a rebuttal to the USDA's Food Pyramid or My Plate, except instead of simply having an unsubstantiated list of food groups and serving suggestions, we provide a set of guidelines on what foods to eat, minimize, and totally avoid.

THE STORM CLOUD

First, let's define the goal. We'll make the assumption that yours is similar to ours: to live a long, happy, productive, disease-free life.

CrossFit founder Greg Glassman describes health as a continuum ranging from sickness to optimal fitness, with everything in between representing various degrees of illness to wellness.

On the extreme end, a poor diet can cause heart disease, cancer, type 2 diabetes, autoimmune conditions, hormone imbalances, and depression. Less severe but still undesirable conditions include acne, low energy, poor sleep, and weight gain.

Think of these ailments combined into an ominous storm cloud. For some of us, that dark cloud might have already moved overhead and is pouring down a host of medical problems. Or perhaps you sense a storm brewing on the horizon. We hope you're currently experiencing clear skies and want to implement preventive measures. But whatever your current climate, you need protection.

BUILDING AN UMBRELLA

THE HANDLE

Naturally, one of the best ways to shelter yourself from a storm is with an umbrella. An umbrella consists of a handle, ribs, and fabric. Similarly, so should your diet. For our figurative umbrella, the handle represents the Primal/paleo lifestyle and the modern science that supports it. Together, they give us the confidence that makes intuitive sense.

It's something we can believe in, that we can grab on to and posture overhead in a confusing world made up of conflicting fads, diet prescriptions, and marketing noise.

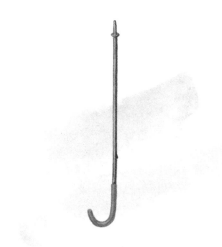

In the last decade, study upon study affirms the health benefits of a natural, nutrient-dense, low-glycemic diet that the Primal/paleo diet affords. The healing benefits include increased energy, weight loss, improved muscle tone, relief from joint pain, lowered blood pressure, reduced liver fat, and improved insulin sensitivity. The substantiating research continues to build as people who switch to a Primal/paleo diet are seeing outstanding results in virtually all health markers.

Now, let's add a few ribs to our umbrella to give it some structure.

THE RIBS

The ribs of our umbrella represent our nutritional priorities. They'll lead us to the best Primal choices and away from what we call "agents of disease." Instead of listing the thousands of foods you "can eat"—without compelling evidence as to why they should be included or excluded—we'll focus on the five nutritional priorities that establish what to embrace, what to minimize, and what to completely avoid.

1. Eat nutrient-dense, whole foods
2. Eliminate grains and legumes
3. Minimize sugar and moderate total carbohydrate intake
4. Know your fats, good from bad
5. Shop for the best

Rib #1: Eat Nutrient-Dense, Whole Foods

Hard to argue that fresh meat, fruit, and veggies pack a greater nutritional punch than those processed for a long shelf life. We're talking nutrient-dense foods sourced directly from the land, the kind available throughout most of human evolution, when those were the only things considered food.

These same basic foods occupy the exterior of your grocery store, where the electrical outlets are located, because they are fresh and in many cases need refrigerating or freezing. High-quality, whole foods are also found at farmers markets (and directly at the farm!). This is not to say that any and all processing is bad, because in a sense cooking is processing—and obviously we are all for cooking. We're just implying that the majority of your food should start as fresh, unprocessed, and unrefined. Whole foods that have been minimally processed through preserving, pressing, fermenting, or drying and grinding are perfectly healthy, too.

As for agents of disease, these would be foods that are far removed from their natural state—resembling nothing our healthy ancestors ate. In fact, when certain processed foods found their way into the indigenous diets of non-industrialized societies, the health of its citizens steadily began to decline. So, good health is as much about what you eat as what you don't.

Think of a high-performance car. If a substance in the fuel causes the car's engine to malfunction, the first thing you're going to do is remove that substance, right? Seeking a remedy by adding anything else to the fuel just doesn't make sense. Your body is the same way. If you are eating something that makes you ill, you must remove the offending item before you can return to good health.

As dramatic as this might sound, much of the foodstuff Americans (and others in the industrialized world) eat and drink on a daily basis are loaded with toxins. Some of the toxins are harmful to us in any quantity. And others are toxic simply by virtue of the dose, meaning it's within our body's experience to remain healthy when exposed to small amounts of certain items. But in larger doses, we become ill.

Rib #2: Eliminate Grains and Legumes

Grains pretty much fall into the class that is toxic in any amount. We know them as wheat, barley, oats, rice, corn, rye, and so forth. We consume them in the products we all know and love, like breads, pastas, cereals, coatings on fried foods, and all manner of pastries and desserts. Grains are hidden in vast amounts of processed foods, and you can bet that most anything you buy from a convenience store or the interior of your grocery store will contain them.

But wait, don't grains come from plants? Technically, yes. But they are actually the seeds of grasses, and under the Primal/paleo definition don't fall neatly within the definition of an edible plant. For our Paleolithic ancestors, grains were virtually inaccessible. Eating them would have required large amounts of time and energy to gather the tiny seeds in any reasonable quantity, remove their hulls, and then soak or cook them to make them edible, a chore that would have burned more calories and fuel than it would have created. Simply put, grains were just too problematic to consume in primal times.

We're now learning that grains are problematic to our health as well. It turns out by evolutionary design. Grains try to protect themselves from being eaten, with an objective to germinate and grow into more grass, which makes perfect sense. Since they can't run or fight back like other prey might, they defend themselves with a manner of chemical warfare with substances collectively known as antinutrients.

Antinutrients such as phytates bind to important vitamins and minerals, which prevents their absorption in our bodies. This is a likely factor in nutritional deficiencies in nations that rely heavily on grain consumption. Quite literally, eating grains leaves us overfed yet undernourished. Possibly worse yet are gliadin proteins, such as gluten and other grain lectins, that can wreak even more havoc on our digestive systems, ultimately causing systemic problems.

Researchers estimate that we all, to some degree, experience adverse reactions to gluten and other gliadin proteins. For some, the reactions are severe enough to warrant medical treatment and lifelong dietary restrictions. For others, the reactions are subclinical. You may recall getting a bloated belly after meals, the occasional sore throat, or an arthritis flareup—generally minor issues that are driven by the continual consumption of proinflammatory, immune- and digestion-compromising foods.

What's more, gluten intolerances, allergies, or sensitivities are diagnosed in millions of Americans every year. Eating grains cause these and other autoimmune conditions, the result of the body attempting to attack offending proteins, but in the process, also attacking its own healthy cells. Rheumatoid arthritis, celiac disease, ulcerative colitis, psoriasis, and Hashimoto's thyroiditis are some of the more well-known autoimmune conditions.

Lectin is another toxin in grains. This sugar-binding protein inhibits the intestine from fully absorbing nutrients, thus creating, you guessed it, more autoimmune problems. Processing and cooking grains help reduce some of these compounds that make us sick, but they are never fully eliminated.

And finally, a word on legumes (beans, soy, lentils, peas, peanuts). They actually offer slightly more nutritional value than grains, and have lower levels of the objectionable lectins and glutens. But there's no good reason to make legumes a part of your diet. They are primarily carbohydrates and contribute to excess insulin production.

Rib #3: Minimize Sugar Intake, Moderate Total Carbohydrate Intake

When we speak of sugar and carbohydrates, we are essentially talking about two sides of the same coin. In most of its forms, sugar breaks down in the body as independent molecules of fructose and glucose, generally about fifty-fifty, while starchy carbs break down into just glucose.

Sugar and carbs are the type of toxins we refer to as "dose specific," since they are within our body's experience to handle well. Indeed, natural carbs and sugar, such as those found in tubers and fruits, qualify as nutrient-dense, whole-food plants. Paul Jaminet, PhD, co-author of *The Perfect Health Diet*, estimates that hunter-gatherers consumed diets made up of 10 to 20 percent carbohydrates by calorie—far less than the USDA's recommendation of 45 to 65 percent carbohydrate intake as outlined in the Dietary Guidelines for Americans, published in 2010.

While the body can well tolerate moderate amounts of carbohydrates and sugar, chronically elevated levels of blood sugar and insulin (which is secreted to process the blood sugar) are toxic and inflammatory to our bodies. Sugars have the potential to bind with dietary proteins and lipids, causing oxidation that in turn produces groups of molecules known as AGEs (Advanced Glycation End-products). AGEs are responsible for generating free radicals that cause further inflammation, and are known to contribute to several diseases, most notably cardiovascular disease. Fructose is especially susceptible to oxidation; it also puts a burden on your liver. For these reasons, it's especially important to limit dietary fructose.

If weight loss is important to you, the intake of sugar and carbs are of special note. Our bodies are hardwired to store excess carbs as fat to be sourced as fuel later. This is why any diet that successfully promotes weight loss must also successfully mitigate constantly elevated blood sugar and insulin. Otherwise, the "later" purpose that the fat was stored for will never materialize, and we will simply store more fat instead of find the delicate balance of storing and burning.

So, how many carbs should you consume? Most people will experience a reduction in excess body fat by consuming an average of 50 to 100 grams of total carbohydrates per day. If you are already at your ideal weight, 150 grams per day represents maintenance. More than 150 grams puts you into a potential fat accumulation zone; exceeding 300 grams per day—the recommendation of conventional wisdom's grain-based diet—puts you into a danger zone of elevated disease risk. Of course, there is never a perfect one-size-fits-all plan, but this is a good rule of thumb. Some people may prefer to be on fewer carbs per day, and it is also possible to do well on more than 150 (depending on the type of carb and your activity level), but the majority of experts in the evolutionary health movement recommend consuming no more than 150 grams of total carbs per day to promote optimum health and weight management.

Of those 50 to 150 grams per day, we aim to keep the sugar amount as low as possible. A few pieces of fruit and the naturally occurring sugar in generous servings of vegetables is plenty of sugar to fuel your daily metabolic needs. Paleo advocate Mat Lalonde, a research biochemist at Harvard University, recommends limiting fructose to 50 grams per day, citing observational studies consistently showing that populations consuming greater than that amount experience problems with blood sugar control. To learn more, we recommend checking out the Primal Blueprint Carbohydrate Curve at MarksDailyApple.com.

We typically fall somewhere in the range of 75 to 150 grams of carbohydrates per day, but find that having one day a week when we allow a higher carbohydrate intake (as much as double the normal amounts) works for us. Not only does the flexibility help keep us sane, but we feel that the higher carb day helps us to recover after several days of good exercise and can have beneficial effects on our respective metabolisms. The point is, we don't want to make carbs out to be an enemy. The way we eat carbohydrates is in moderation, but it's really about understanding how our bodies treat them and figuring out how many are right for you and your goals. We use some of the more natural, less refined sweeteners when possible. But ultimately sugar is sugar (or more accurately, glucose and fructose are glucose and fructose), so we strive to be responsible about our intake. Also keep in mind that if you are struggling with weight loss and want to make progress, limiting your carb intake is the most direct and effective path. The less insulin you produce on a daily basis, the better you will become at burning off excess body fat.

Rib #4: Know Your Fats, Good From Bad

Fat has taken the rap for many of today's health problems, so this is one principle where we feel we must be begrudgingly concise. In his books, *Why We Get Fat* and *Good Calories, Bad Calories*, Gary Taubes exposes the flawed science and reckless governmental policy that has demonized dietary fat for the last half-century, essentially changing the paradigm that dietary fat makes us sick and obese. This is not the place to go down the rabbit hole on the misguided conventional wisdom about fat, but we highly recommend investigating Taubes' work. Evidence suggests that our healthy and robust primal ancestors consumed between 28 to 58 percent fat by calorie. The majority of this fat would have been saturated animal fat. The sad truth is, our fears about saturated fat steer us directly toward health-compromising grains.

Not only has saturated fat never been conclusively linked to heart disease or any other health risk, but saturated fat is essential to life. Saturated fats make up half of our cell membrane structure and aid in immune function. They are essential to brain health and deliver fat-soluble vitamins that can't be obtained any other way.

The good news is a Primal/paleo diet includes ample saturated fat, monounsaturated fat, and some polyunsaturated fats. Since we need not worry about the saturated fat content in the plants and animals we eat, we can add variety and purchase cuts of meat that are less expensive.

Polyunsaturated fats (PUFAs) are the caveat in this whole fat discussion. There are two main types as they apply to what we eat, and those are omega-3 and omega-6 polyunsaturated fats. At the molecular level, saturated fats present no double bonds, but unsaturated fats do. The numbers correspond to the number and position of the molecule's carbon bonds.

Omega-3 is the polyunsaturated fat that is a precursor to anti-inflammatory type actions in our bodies. It's received extensive good press lately, and rightfully so. Conversely, omega-6 in large doses promotes more inflammatory type actions. These two fats are essential (meaning we must obtain them from diet; they are not manufactured internally), and ideally balanced in a 1:1 ratio, very close to the ratio of our ancestors' diet. Unfortunately, the widespread use of refined oils has us exposed to exorbitant amounts of omega-6. Typical examples of high omega-6 refined oils are soybean oil, peanut oil, corn oil, and canola oil. Today, it's estimated that the standard American diet delivers an omega-6:omega-3 ratio of around 20:1! Hence, it's urgent to cut your consumption of chemically altered trans and partially hydrogenated fats as well as vegetable oils, and boost your intake of healthy omega-3 rich foods.

Unsaturated fats are also unstable and prone to oxidation, especially at high heat. This gives another thumbs up to saturated fat, which is much more stable. On the Primal/paleo diet, we obtain ample omega-3 from oily, cold-water fish and grass-fed beef, and omega-6 in some animal fats and sensible nut consumption. Many nuts are high in omega-6; they are on the proverbial "enjoy moderately" list. So, to reduce omega-6 in your Primal treats, we're very proud to say that we've pioneered new baking methods that do not use almond flour.

Rib #5: Shop For The Best

Where budget allows, consider the quality of your meat, vegetables, and other grocery items. Get beyond just the labels—organic, free-range, etc.—and get to know where your food is sourced. Ideally, animals should eat a species-specific diet and live in a clean environment that allows for natural mobility instead of forced confinement. Wild fish and seafood, grass-fed beef and dairy, pastured pork, pastured and free-ranging poultry and eggs are preferred. Wild game is excellent. Include local, in-season produce whenever possible, and try to moderate your intake of remote, conventionally grown, out of season produce. See the resources section for reputable online purveyors of quality products.

THE FABRIC

We now have the handle (eat plants and animals) and the ribs (the research that supports why). But when we look up, we still see the sky. We need one final piece to complete our umbrella: the fabric, that is, the actual foods we will eat.

MEAT AND EGGS Beef, pork, lamb, bison, poultry, eggs, seafood and shellfish, game meats, organ meats, and other less common animal meats

VEGETABLES Mostly non-starchy. Of the starchy veggies, we use potatoes, sweet potatoes (and yams), celery root, cassava root (tapioca), plantains, and winter squash

NUTS AND APPROVED FATS Enjoy nuts moderately; macadamias are the best for their monounsaturated content (no concerns about omega-6:omega-3 imbalance). Non-dairy cooking fats include tallow, duck fat, lard, olive oil, high oleic sunflower oil, coconut oil, and palm oil and palm shortening

FRUIT AND ADDED NATURAL SWEETENERS Berries and cherries make the best fruit choices. We also use coconut sugar, honey, maple syrup, and fruit juice concentrates

DAIRY Grass-fed (and raw when possible), heavy cream, butter, and cheeses

DAIRY

FRUIT & NATURAL SWEETENERS

NUTS & APPROVED FATS

VEGETABLES

MEAT & EGGS

This is what we'll implement to keep us out of the bad weather. It's also the template we apply to our recipes. The tenets here comprise what we believe are 80 to 90 percent of the actionable steps of a good Primal/paleo diet. (This book does not address any specific autoimmune or gut-healing protocols and respective food restrictions/eliminations.)

HOME RUN RECIPES AND WINNING RESULTS

In the world where we live today, eating nutrient-dense, whole foods and avoiding or minimizing the agents of disease requires a real investment in time and money. It's with that in mind that we feel that the need to get a great, enjoyable, tasty result out of your efforts is that much more important.

We've experimented, tested, tasted, made mistakes, and fine-tuned so you don't have to. In many cases, we set out to do things that have never been done before. Where we failed to get the intended result we had to look at the bright side. As Thomas Edison reminds us, we didn't fail; we simply found ten thousand ways that did not work. What remains are a collection of foolproof, home run recipes that will let all the money and time you spent on your food shine on the plate.

Portion Sizes

As for calories, they do matter but not necessarily in the ways we generally think. It isn't just an "in versus out" or "burning off" calories issue. What happens to the calories we eat depends on what kind of macronutrient they are (protein, fat, or carbohydrate) and what state our body is in when we consume them (resting all day, post workout, etc.). For example, carbohydrates can be stored as muscle glycogen (energy for muscles) after a workout, but stored as body fat after a day of inactivity.

Total calories do play a role, but eating the appropriate foods for our bodies help regulate our hunger so that we don't overeat. One of the most liberating features of a Primal/paleo diet is how satiating food becomes. Typically, once you start eating within a Primal/paleo template, you don't have to count your daily calorie intake at all because your body "knows" what and how much it needs.

Also on a Primal/paleo diet, your body can receive signals to burn fat and becomes "fat adapted" by up-regulating bodily functions involved in accessing and burning fat for energy. A lower-carbohydrate, higher-fat diet can reteach your body to better burn fat for fuel. Fat is the preferred fuel of the human metabolism and has been for most of human evolution, but the high-carb, standard American diet makes us dependent on a fresh source of sugar (carbs) every few hours and thwarts our ability to mobilize and oxidize fat for fuel.

Speaking like our body has a mind of its own really isn't much of a stretch. Our accumulated body fat is a living organ in and of itself. Without proper signaling, the fat mass will defend itself (that spare tire wants to stay there believing it is in your own best interest) against your efforts to lose it. If you aren't seeing the results you'd like without counting calories, or if you feel the palatability of food is keeping you from reaching your goals, restricting carbohydrates further can turbocharge your success with fat reduction.

Pass the Woolly Mammoth, Please

And finally, we aren't after a reenactment of the past here. Truth is, almost nothing we have available today is identical to the foodstuffs available during Paleolithic times. The majority of available foods today are but analogs to the types of things that were eaten by our ancestors. To that end, we apply the "template" idea—that is, eating in a way that is *informed* by our healthy predecessors, but not *identical*. That includes the ingredients we choose as well as how we apply them in preparation.

Some might disagree with our approach. The argument goes that fare that resembles anything that we typically think of as a comfort food or an indulgence—even if we've removed all or most of the unhealthy agents—provide a psychological crutch, and therefore should be strictly off-limits. We disagree.

The problem with this argument is that it implies that anyone who enjoys an occasional treat has no self-control or is unaware of other factors in their decision making. We firmly believe that your diet should not be stressful, and enjoying treats with the decision influenced by nutritional priorities is the healthiest way to live, physically and mentally. This is what we mean when we talk about mindful eating. If, however, you feel that you are exhibiting serious compulsive or addictive behavior with food, extra steps beyond simply understanding context could be in order and professional help is advised.

So in the end, it really just becomes more about creating a healthy mindset and a workable lifestyle that fits within the Primal/paleo guidelines and not about replicating the past exactly as it once was tens of thousands of years ago. If we can get the results we want—feeling, looking, and performing well—and still include the flavors, textures, aromas, and experiences we enjoy, we see no reason not to. With this approach, we really can have the best of both worlds.

THE 80/20 RULE

Thirty-day challenges or elimination diets have been associated with Primal/paleo eating for a while now. These challenges give you a set of rules to follow and a time frame in which to comply. The idea is to try and go to somewhat of an extreme in hopes of lasting change. The hosts of such challenges may even admit that the challenge is more stringent than what would be appropriate in everyday life.

We can honestly see the appeal for someone who does well with structure and looks at the challenge as a tangible goal; we know they can work. If a challenge introduced you to the Primal/paleo lifestyle, or you're on a challenge now, we applaud your desire to create lasting change. We do, however, see potential problems with some of the more radical challenges and believe there are better ways to create change.

Beware of challenges asking you to be especially strict, as they can set you up for disappointment when you give into life. Any little slip up puts you back at square one, and shoot, as long as you're there, how easy is it to consider binging for a while before starting over? And then for some, trying to avoid a particular food seems to make it that much more difficult to resist! Others might have to look for an unobstructed social schedule with no family events, holidays, or travel that could tempt them. That unobstructed time will likely never come. We all have busy lives that can get in the way, despite careful attention and preparation, and that shouldn't be something to feel stressed or guilty about.

What's more, 100 percent compliance may not be any better than 80 percent compliance. We wholeheartedly believe that real, permanent change doesn't come from an all-or-nothing attitude; it comes from consistency over the long term.

Enter the 80/20 Rule. Now, this is not an invitation to eat 80 percent good stuff and 20 percent junk! Nor is it a suggestion to strive for just 80 percent and see where you land. Instead, strive to adhere to the ribs of the umbrella—find your foods, moderate carb intake, avoid grains, etc.—knowing that within these guidelines, your efforts will deliver excellence, even if you give in now and then.

With an 80/20 attitude, real life fits in comfortably with your dietary goals, so when (not if) something less than perfect comes up, you do the best you can (or choose to do) and then move on. Either way, you still land at excellence.

And lastly, though the recipes provided here give you much healthier options, remember that the sweet treats in this book are still just that: treats. Stay committed to your lifestyle goals, be flexible by using the 80/20 Rule, and you will benefit in the long run. Because if you can bend a little, you will not break entirely.

THE FAT ON DAIRY

For us, dairy falls into a gray area. While it's not technically congruous with what was likely available to our ancient ancestors, the science doesn't conclusively condemn appropriate dairy choices either. This one really falls to personal tolerance and preference. We generally caution people with weight loss goals to emphasize high-fat dairy products and eliminate the more common high-carbohydrate dairy products such as skim milk and fruit-sweetened yogurt.

Butter and cheeses, however, especially raw from pastured, humanely raised dairy animals (cows, sheep, goats) are generally well tolerated, even for those who are lactose intolerant. These high-fat content foods support fat reduction goals. Butter and cheeses contain virtually zero carbohydrate and minimal amounts of lactose. They are rich in healthy fats similar in composition to the fats eaten by our fit predecessors. The only dairy products we use in this book are butter, some heavy cream, and cheeses.

> If you're complying most (not all) of the time, your effort will deliver excellence, even if you give in now and then.

FOR MORE INFORMATION

All of the topics we just discussed could be expounded into full books, and they have. Here's a list of our favorites. Also, see our Resources section on page 268 for a list of websites.

The Primal Blueprint, Mark Sisson
Lights Out: Sleep, Sugar and Survival, T.S. Wiley with Bent Formby
Nourishing Traditions, Sally Fallon with Mary G. Enig
Wheat Belly, William Davis
Perfect Health Diet, Paul Jaminet and Shou-Ching Jaminet
Why We Get Fat, Gary Taubes

PROTEIN

	BEEF	POULTRY	PORK	SEAFOOD
BUDGET	ground beef	ground chicken	ground pork	cod
	sirloin steak	chicken wings	sausage	canned sardines
	chuck roast	chicken thighs	shoulder/butt	canned tuna
	shoulder	drumsticks	bacon	canned salmon
	tri-tip	ground turkey		mussels
		turkey legs		
		eggs		
SLOW & LOW	chuck roast	whole chicken	shanks	
	shoulder	drumsticks	loin	
	short ribs		shoulder/butt	
	brisket		picnic	
	shanks		ribs	
			belly	
QUICK	ground beef	ground chicken	pork tenderloin	tuna
	flank steak	chicken breasts	chops	salmon
	skirt steak	chicken thighs	bacon	shrimp
	hanger steak	chicken wings	Canadian bacon	mahi mahi
	flat iron steak	ground turkey		scallops
	sirloin steak	eggs		clams
	rib-eye			mussels
	tenderloin			crawfish

OTHER PROTEINS

Lamb, game meats, all other fish and shellfish, dairy (if you eat it), and any other animal protein you can get your hands on.

CARBOHYDRATES

GREEN PLANTAINS

Green plantains are starchy marvels of nature. Extremely affordable, this giant banana-like fruit is often used as a vegetable and goes well beyond traditional Cuban and Hispanic cuisine. If you let the green plantain sit and ripen, you can slice it and fry it up in butter for a wonderfully sweet treat.

ROOT VEGETABLES

Celery root (which is literally the root ball of a type of celery), cassava (tapioca), jicama, and beets are among our favorites.

WINTER SQUASH

Butternut squash and pumpkin are the two main winter squashes we use in this book. Fresh or canned will work just fine.

POTATOES

We use waxy potato varieties, including red skin and Yukon gold. When buying, look for thin, smooth skin, not papery and rough.

SWEET POTATOES & YAMS

Yams and sweet potatoes—white or orange—either kind is A-OK with us.

POTATO FLOUR

Potato flour is finely ground, dehydrated potatoes. When buying, look for an off-white colored powder. Potato flour should not be confused with potato starch. We prefer to use Bob's Red Mill brand.

POTATO STARCH

Potato starch is starch extracted from the potato tuber. When buying, look for a vivid white powder, as potato starch should not be confused for potato flour. We recommend ENER-G brand potato starch, which they call "potato starch flour."

COCONUT FLOUR

Coconut flour is finely ground, dried coconut meat. It's high in fiber and naturally gluten-free. We like Let's Do Organic brand and Tropical Traditions brand.

TAPIOCA FLOUR

Tapioca flour, sometimes labeled tapioca starch, is the starch found in the root vegetable cassava, also known as manioc or yuca, but not yucca. Tapioca flour is naturally gluten-free and versatile, giving crunch to crackers and crusts and providing a beautifully tender crumb in muffins and cakes. We prefer to use the ENER-G and NOW Foods brands. We do not recommend Bob's Red Mill, as it can have an off-putting taste.

FATS & OILS

BUTTER

We rely on butter as our main fat source in this book. It has a negligible amount of lactose, but for those with severe sensitivities, we recommend substituting with cultured butter, clarified butter, or any other fats on this list when cooking. For baking we recommend palm shortening.

PALM SHORTENING

Palm shortening is palm oil that's had some of its unsaturated fats removed. It has a firm but pliable texture, a high smoke point, and a neutral flavor. This is a non-hydrogenated, trans-fat-free product and should not be confused with conventional vegetable shortening or palm oil. We like Tropical Traditions and Spectrum brands.

COCONUT OIL

There are many varieties of coconut oil. We prefer to cook and bake with the expeller-pressed variety because of its neutral taste. Tropical Traditions brand cannot be beat for quality or price. Coconut oil makes a great substitute for butter in the muffin recipes.

COCONUT BUTTER

Also called coconut cream concentrate, coconut butter is puréed dried coconut meat. You can make it yourself (you'll find a recipe for it on our website, Health-Bent.com), or buy it online and in most natural/whole food stores.

COCONUT MILK

We prefer to use Thai Kitchens simply because we haven't found a brand that's thicker or richer.

TALLOW & SUCH

Though we don't specifically call for the more uncommon animal fats like beef tallow, lard, and duck fat, they're absolutely fantastic for cooking. We highly recommend them.

BACON

Yes, yes, bacon is a protein, but it only seems natural to discuss one of its most endearing qualities—its fat renderings. Once your bacon is cooked, pour off and save the liquid fat to use for pan-searing and sautéing.

EXTRA VIRGIN OLIVE OIL

This is a staple in most homes, so there's nothing new to report on this oil, except maybe that we only use it in its raw form. Cooking or heating really isn't a great idea with this stuff. We just use it as a finishing oil and in salad dressings.

HIGH OLEIC SUNFLOWER OIL

Made from non-genetically modified sunflower seeds, this oil has a favorable monounsaturated fat content, while boasting a very low polyunsaturated fat content (mostly omega-3). Neutral in flavor, it's the perfect oil for vinaigrette and mayonnaise making. We use Spectrum brand.

SWEETENERS

We use sweeteners that are as natural as possible and stay mindful of the amounts we consume.

COCONUT SUGAR

A relatively inexpensive, unrefined natural sweetener, coconut sugar (also called palm sugar) is made from the sap of the coconut palm. This sweetener is traditional to the cuisine of Southeast Asia. You can find it online, at most natural/whole food grocery stores, and in some conventional grocery stores. It tastes similar to brown sugar.

HONEY

You won't find much honey in our recipes. When we do use it, we prefer local varieties. We don't recommend substituting honey in any baking recipes that don't call for it, as honey can cause some sweet treats to over brown.

MAPLE SYRUP

We prefer and pretty much exclusively use Grade B maple syrup—it's cheaper and more flavorful than the Grade A variety.

100 PERCENT FRUIT JAM

This is just jam or jelly that's been sweetened with fruit, usually apple juice concentrate, instead of refined cane sugar. You can find this type of jam in various flavors, at conventional and natural/whole food grocery stores.

APPLE JUICE CONCENTRATE

You can find this in the freezer section of almost every grocery store. You can also find other juice flavor varieties and combinations. Feel free to experiment.

APPLESAUCE

Most of our sweet recipes call for unsweetened applesauce, which you can find at almost any grocery store. We also use fruit sweetened applesauce. Instead of sugar, it is sweetened with fruit concentrates and purées, most commonly apple, but you can also find it sweetened with cherry, mango, peach, and berry.

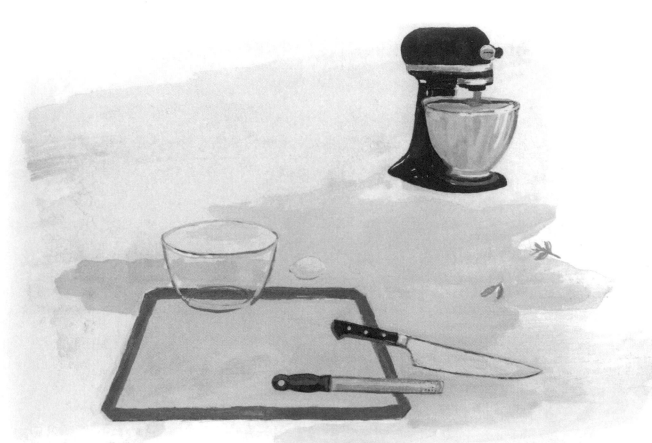

TOOLS & EQUIPMENT

No kiwi slicers or banana peelers here. These are the essentials. If one of these things broke or met a tumultuous ending, we'd immediately go out and replace them, they're that essential.

SHARP KNIVES

With knives, you get what you pay for. We use Japanese layered steel knives. You really only need a few knives in your kitchen: a utility knife, a pairing knife, and an 8- to 10-inch chef's knife, depending on how big your hands are and what you're comfortable with. Shopping for knives should be like shopping for clothes: you really should see how it fits before buying.

KNIFE SHARPENER

Almost as equally important as a few nice knives is a knife sharpener that can actually attain a razor-sharp edge. Dull knives make for an incredibly unkind cooking experience. We use the Edgemate Professional Sharpening System from GatcoSharpeners.com.

PLASTIC CUTTING BOARDS

Thin, flexible boards are great for cutting and butchering meat, while thicker boards are ideal for fruit and veggie prep. One of the main reasons we love the plastic boards so much is the added bonus of being able to stick them in the dishwasher.

NON-SLIP DRAWER LINER

Cut a rectangle of liner a few inches smaller than your cutting board and place under the board for a stay-put (and safe) workspace. You can also dampen a paper towel and place it under your cutting board for the same effect.

MANDOLINE

Not absolutely essential, but sure nice to have around. We own a cheap fixed-blade mandoline. Fancy-pants versions exist, with interchangeable blades and thicknesses, but they're bulky to store.

POTS & PANS

Same rule applies to pots and pans as to knives: a few high-quality pieces will get any job done. Here are basic must-haves.

> 12- or 14-inch fry pan
> 4-quart sauté pan with lid
> cast-iron skillet
> 3-quart sauce pot with lid
> enamel cast iron dutch oven
> large roasting pan with rack

BAKING SHEETS

It's all about the basics when it comes to baking sheets, also commonly called sheet pans or cookie pans. We pretty much stick to rectangular ones that we can buy at our local restaurant supply store. They're very affordable and durable.

PARCHMENT PAPER OR SILICONE PAT

Though not technically equipment, maybe more of a sorta-kinda-halfway tool, buying parchment paper or investing in a silicone pat is absolutely necessary for creating beautifully browned and easy-to-remove baked goods.

MIXING BOWLS

Duh, we know. But glass bowls are worth noting. Plastic wrap sticks beautifully to them, and they're microwave-safe, oven-safe, and freezer-safe, which makes them easy to mix stuff in, store food in, cook in, and serve in. Plus there's the added bonus that you can see through them, helping you see if you've mixed, whipped, stirred, and combined thoroughly.

FINE MESH STRAINER

For straining homemade stock and egg-based desserts. Look for a tightly woven metal "net," not a pasta strainer.

COOKIE SCOOP

These babies are absolute must-haves. Not only do they work well for scooping cookie dough, but they're great for perfectly portioned, uniform meatballs.

BISCUIT CUTTER

Sometimes called ring molds, biscuit cutters can be purchased in sets of various sizes or just one-by-one. You don't need anything too fancy, just a standard 3- or 4-inch metal circle will do.

MICROPLANE ZESTER

The hands-down best way to get the zest (sans pith) off a piece of citrus. You can also use it to grate fresh nutmeg and cheese, if you're into that sort of thing.

FOOD PROCESSOR

Though an expensive food chopper-upper, it's definitely worth having when you're prepping large batches of vegetables.

STAND MIXER

There is no amount of hand mixing or whipping that can ever compete with the performance of an electric stand mixer. If you want perfectly creamed, blended, and aerated confections, which we all do, it's an absolutely essential piece of baking equipment.

BLENDER

They come in variations galore. Look for a high-powered, commercial-style blender like Vitamix. It'll cost a pretty penny, but they blend circles around the cheaper, less powerful ones.

IMMERSION BLENDER

Also called a hand blender or stick blender, these are great for puréeing small batches of soups and vegetables straight in the pot, so there's no need to transfer the liquid concoction from pot to blender and back to pot again; you can just blend and serve.

SQUEEZE BOTTLES

Think mustard and ketchup bottles. They're absolutely essential for making mayonnaise. We fill them with oils, like olive and high oleic sunflower. You can find them in a variety of sizes at most grocery and restaurant supply stores.

RESTAURANT SUPPLY STORES

Everything you need, you'll find here. Don't be afraid of these places. Most are open to the public and you'll wonder why you hadn't thought of this sooner. Whisks, spatulas, measuring spoons and cups, scoops, cutters, food storage bins, even pots, pans, and knives. Not only are the prices unbeatable, but it's commercial quality. If this stuff is good enough for a fancy gourmet restaurant kitchen, it's good enough for us humble home cooks.

STOCKING THE KITCHEN

Being prepared for not being prepared, that's the name of the game here. It's what stocking a kitchen is all about. So maybe you didn't make a meal plan this week, or maybe you never make a meal plan. The beauty of having a well-stocked kitchen is that none of that matters. Keep these ingredients on hand, and you'll always have what you need to make your taste buds and tummy happy.

PANTRY	FRIDGE	FREEZER

PROTEINS

canned sardines and tuna, jerky, powdered gelatin	ground meat, smoked salmon, chicken breasts and/or thighs, raw and hard-boiled eggs, bacon or sausage	ground meat, sausage, bacon, seafood, cheap cuts (shoulder, shank, ribs, etc.), flank or skirt steaks that easily fast-thaw and quick-cook

PRODUCE

sweet potatoes, waxy potatoes, plantains, onions, garlic, winter squash, root veggies	seasonal fruit, celery, carrots, bell peppers, mushrooms, lettuce, kale, spinach, cucumbers, ginger, green onions, avocados, fresh herbs	homemade stock, squash purée, chopped spinach, pitted cherries, chopped mango, peeled bananas, apple juice concentrate and other juice concentrates

FATS & OILS

coconut oil, palm shortening, coconut butter	butter, duck fat (for special occasions), nuts and nut butters, high oleic sunflower oil, extra virgin olive oil	

SWEETENERS

coconut sugar, honey, molasses, chocolate chips		

SPICES & SUCH

cinnamon, nutmeg, cloves, allspice, cocoa powder, vanilla extract, ginger, red pepper flakes, cumin, coriander, powdered onion, garlic, curry powder, Italian seasoning, chili powder, baking soda, baking powder	maple syrup, 100 percent fruit jam, curry paste, mango chutney, Sriracha or chili garlic sauce, hot sauce, yellow mustard, Dijon mustard, Worcestershire sauce, capers, horseradish, ketchup, roasted red peppers, olives, banana peppers, jalapeño peppers	

CANS, BOTTLES & BOXES

store-bought stock, chipotle peppers in adobo, canned tomatoes (sauce, crushed, and diced), tomato paste, olives, artichokes, coconut milk, coconut flour, tapioca flour, potato flour, potato starch, canned pumpkin, canned crushed pineapple, unsweetened applesauce, vinegars, wheat-free, reduced sodium soy sauce (or coconut aminos)		

RISE 'N' SHINE

HAZELNUT COFFEE PANCAKES

MAKES ABOUT 10 PANCAKES

A standard cup o' joe packs a tasty punch to a weekend breakfast favorite.

½   cup tapioca flour

½   cup coconut flour

1   teaspoon baking soda

1   teaspoon baking powder

¼   cup hazelnuts, skinned and finely chopped

¼   teaspoon coffee extract

1   cup brewed coffee, cooled

4   eggs

Butter for pan

Maple syrup

1 Whisk together tapioca flour, coconut flour, baking soda, and baking powder in a bowl. Add the chopped hazelnuts and whisk to combine.

2 In a large bowl, whisk together coffee extract, coffee, and eggs.

3 Whisk the dry ingredients into the wet ingredients.

4 Melt a few tablespoons of butter over medium heat in a griddle pan or skillet. Working in batches, pour or ladle the pancake batter onto the griddle. Let the pancake cook about 2 minutes until little bubbles form on top; that's when you know it's time to flip it. Cook the other side for another 2 minutes or until browned.

5 Serve with maple syrup.

STRAWBERRY SHORTCAKE WAFFLES

SERVES 4

Grain-free waffles topped with fresh strawberries and cream.

FOR THE STRAWBERRY WAFFLES

- ½ cup tapioca flour
- ½ cup coconut flour
- ¾ teaspoon baking powder
- ½ cup butter, melted
- ¼ cup 100 percent fruit strawberry jam
- ½ cup strawberry sweetened applesauce
- 1 teaspoon vanilla extract
- 4 eggs
- ½ teaspoon salt

FOR THE SHORTCAKE ASSEMBLY

- 1 pint strawberries
- 3 tablespoons 100 percent fruit strawberry jam
- ½ cup heavy cream
- 1 teaspoon vanilla extract

1 Preheat waffle iron.

2 In a bowl, stir together tapioca flour, coconut flour, and baking powder.

3 In a large bowl, whisk butter, ¼ cup strawberry jam, applesauce, vanilla extract, eggs, and salt.

4 Whisk the dry ingredients into the wet ingredients.

5 Scoop about a third of the batter into the waffle iron. Cook until the waffle has browned, about 4 minutes. Continue cooking the waffles in batches until you've run out of batter.

6 Meanwhile, slice the strawberries and place them in a bowl. Mix with 2 tablespoons strawberry jam.

7 In another large bowl, whisk together heavy cream, the remaining tablespoon of strawberry jam, and vanilla extract until the mixture holds its shape. Do not over whisk.

8 To serve, break each waffle into quadrants. Each serving is composed of three waffle quadrants. Place one quadrant on a plate, top with strawberries and whipped cream. Repeat with the remaining two waffle quadrants. Repeat with the remaining three servings.

CHERRY ALMOND STREUSEL MUFFINS

MAKES 12

A perfect brunch muffin that hits all the right spots and textures—sweet, nutty, crunchy, and fruity. Don't bother with fresh; use frozen, already pitted cherries.

½ cup coconut flour

½ cup tapioca flour

1 teaspoon baking soda

1 teaspoon ground cinnamon

1 teaspoon ground cardamom

½ cup coconut oil, melted

⅓ cup coconut sugar

4 eggs

½ cup unsweetened applesauce

1 teaspoon almond extract

1 cup frozen cherries, chopped

Honey Nut Crunch (page 52), unbaked

1 Preheat oven to 350°F. Line a standard muffin tin with paper liners.

2 In a large bowl, whisk together coconut flour, tapioca flour, baking soda, cinnamon, and cardamom.

3 In another large bowl, whisk together coconut oil and coconut sugar. Whisk in eggs, one at a time, making sure each egg is thoroughly mixed in before adding the next. Whisk in applesauce and almond extract. Fold in cherries.

4 Whisk the dry ingredients into the wet ingredients.

5 Divide batter among the lined muffin cups.

6 Place about 2 tablespoons of Honey Nut Crunch on top of each muffin, and bake until the muffins are golden brown, about 20 minutes.

HONEY NUT CRUNCH

MAKES ABOUT 2 CUPS

Make it and bake it, and you've got a grab 'n' go morning granola or midday snack. Use this recipe as a topping for the Cherry Almond Streusel Muffins or cut up some fresh, ripe fruit, then pack on the Honey Nut Crunch and bake for an easy fruit crisp.

1   cup nuts (almonds, pistachios, pecans, and macadamias all work)

2   tablespoons tapioca flour

½   teaspoon salt

1   teaspoon ground cinnamon

¼   cup honey

¼   cup cold butter, cut into teaspoon-size cubes

1 In the bowl of a food processor, add nuts, tapioca flour, salt, cinnamon, and honey.

2 Add in butter one or two chunks at a time, pulsing the food processor until you've developed a rough, chunky texture.

3 For granola, evenly spread the mixture on a silicone pat or a baking sheet lined with parchment paper. Bake at 350°F for 12 minutes.

GINGERBREAD MUFFINS

MAKES 12

This gingerbread is not shy. The spicy, sweet flavors walk right up to your taste buds and give 'em a firm but friendly handshake.

½ cup coconut flour

½ cup tapioca flour

1 teaspoon baking soda

2 teaspoons powdered ginger

1 teaspoon ground cloves

½ teaspoon ground allspice

½ cup butter, melted

¼ cup coconut sugar

¼ cup molasses

4 eggs

½ cup unsweetened applesauce

1 Preheat oven to 350°F. Line a standard muffin tin with paper liners.

2 In a large bowl, whisk together coconut flour, tapioca flour, baking soda, ginger, cloves, and allspice.

3 In another large bowl, whisk together butter, coconut sugar, and molasses. Whisk in eggs, one at a time, making sure each egg is thoroughly mixed in before adding the next. Whisk in applesauce.

4 Whisk the dry ingredients into the wet ingredients, then fill the lined muffin cups about three-quarters of the way up with batter.

5 Bake until the muffins are golden brown, about 20 minutes.

BISCUITS

MAKES 8

To us, biscuits are the American croissant. Though buttery and flaky in different ways, the texture and flavor are just the same. Megan's mom scratch-made biscuits almost every Saturday morning when Megan was a kid, probably the only way her mom could get her out of bed before noon.

   1   cup tapioca flour

   ⅓   cup coconut flour

   2   teaspoons baking powder

   ½   teaspoon salt

   ½   cup butter, chilled

   1   egg

   ⅓   cup cold water

   Honey Butter (below)

1 Preheat oven to 400°F. Line a baking sheet with a silicone pat or parchment paper.

2 In a large bowl, whisk together tapioca flour, coconut flour, baking powder, and salt.

3 Cut the butter into teaspoon-size chunks. Add the butter to the flour mixture and use your fingers to rub together until mixture looks crumbly and sandy.

4 Add the egg and water. Use your hands to gently mix until ingredients are incorporated.

5 Using your hands, form the dough into round discs and place onto the baking sheet, making sure the biscuits do not touch.

6 Bake until the biscuit bottoms have slightly browned, about 20 to 25 minutes. Serve with Honey Butter.

HONEY BUTTER

MAKES ½ CUP

   ½   cup butter, softened

   2   tablespoons honey

   ½   teaspoon salt

1 Whisk together ingredients until evenly combined.

2 Serve immediately or store in the fridge for up to 2 weeks.

CHUNKY MONKEY MUFFINS

MAKES 12

A classic combination of bananas, walnuts, and chocolate chips. Make sure you use bananas that are brown and spotty. If they're too ripe for eatin', then they're perfect for beatin' — errr, baking with.

½ cup coconut flour

½ cup tapioca flour

1 teaspoon baking soda

½ cup butter, melted

½ cup coconut sugar

1 cup bananas, mashed

1 teaspoon vanilla extract

4 eggs

½ cup chocolate chips

½ cup walnuts, chopped

1 Preheat oven to 350°F. Line a standard muffin tin with paper liners.

2 In a large bowl, whisk together coconut flour, tapioca flour, and baking soda.

3 In another large bowl, whisk together butter, sugar, bananas, vanilla extract, and eggs.

4 Whisk the dry ingredients into the wet ingredients.

5 Gently fold in the chocolate chips and walnuts. Divide batter among the lined muffin cups.

6 Bake until the muffins have puffed and the edges have slightly browned, about 20 minutes.

DAIRY-FREE STRAWBERRY YOGURT

MAKES 4 CUPS

1½ pounds frozen strawberries, 2 tablespoons 100 percent fruit strawberry jam,
4 egg yolks, 1 cup coconut oil

1 Over medium heat, place strawberries and jam in a large sauce pot and heat until they're bubbly and broken down. Place strawberry mixture in a blender and purée until smooth.

2 In the bowl of an electric mixer, whisk egg yolks until pale and fluffy. Slowly pour in the hot strawberry purée and whip on high, until cool. Once the mixture is cool, whisk in coconut oil, 1 tablespoon at a time. Refrigerate at least 4 hours, until the "yogurt" has firmed up.

COWBOY HASHBROWN SKILLET

SERVES 6

A feast for a king...and a cowboy. Chow down on this for breakfast, and it'll keep you going strong all day long.

Butter for the pan

2   green plantains, peeled and grated on a box grater

1   large yellow onion, diced

1   pound fresh Chorizo Sausage (page 266 or store-bought)

6   eggs

2   ripe Haas avocados, diced

Salsa (page 267 or store-bought)

Hot sauce

Salt to taste

1 Preheat oven to 350°F.

2 In an oven-safe or cast-iron skillet, crumble and brown the chorizo. Remove from the pan and reserve.

3 Heat a few tablespoons of butter in a skillet over medium heat. Add in the plantains and onion. Season with salt. Stirring occasionally, cook until browned, about 12 minutes. Add the chorizo back into the pan and stir to combine.

4 Use a spoon to create 6 wells. Crack an egg into each well. Place the skillet in the oven and cook until the eggs are set, about 8 minutes.

5 Carefully remove from the oven, and top with diced avocado, salsa, and a few dashes of hot sauce.

SAUSAGE & EGGS TO GO

MAKES 6

A solid recipe as-is. You could also use this recipe as a base for endless variations. Try sautéing mushrooms and onions or bell peppers and ham, then adding them into whisked eggs.

1 pound Breakfast Sausage (page 264 or store-bought)

6 eggs

1 green onion, sliced

Salt to taste

1 Preheat oven to 350°F.

2 Divide the sausage into 6 portions, and place each into its own individual ramekin. Use your hands to push the sausage around the bottom and up the sides of the ramekin, creating a "crust" for the egg to bake in.

3 Crack an egg into each sausage crust. For a scrambled variation, whisk the eggs before pouring in.

4 Top with a sprinkle of salt and a few slices of green onion.

5 Bake until the eggs are set, about 30 minutes.

WESTERN OMELETTE TO GO

MAKES 6

Standard fare at most breakfast spots, use this recipe to create the same flavors, but in a convenient, ready-to-go package.

6   slices deli ham

6   eggs

2   tablespoons bell pepper, finely chopped

2   tablespoons yellow onion, finely diced

Salt to taste

1 Preheat oven to 350°F.

2 Line a standard muffin tin with ham slices.

3 In a bowl, whisk together eggs, bell pepper, onion, and salt.

4 Pour egg mixture into ham-lined muffin cups.

5 Bake until eggs are set, about 15 to 18 minutes.

CAPRESE BAKED EGGS

MAKES 6

A refined, more grown-up version of the first meal I ever made for Brandon.

Butter for the ramekins

1 cup Pizza Sauce (page 263 or store-bought)

6 eggs

2 tablespoons fresh basil, minced

2 tablespoons extra virgin olive oil

1 teaspoon lemon juice

Salt to taste

1 Preheat oven to 400°F. Generously grease 6 ramekin dishes with butter (to help keep the egg white from sticking to the sides. That's no fun to clean.)

2 Evenly spoon pizza sauce into ramekins. Crack 1 egg into each ramekin.

3 Make the pesto by whisking together the basil, olive oil, lemon juice, and salt. Spoon on top of the eggs.

4 Place ramekins on a baking sheet and bake until the eggs are set, about 18 to 20 minutes.

SMOKED SALMON HASH

SERVES 4

For reasons unbeknownst to us, people actually get tired of eating bacon and eggs for breakfast. So let's shake up the typical morning routine with smoked salmon. You can use either cold-smoked or hot-smoked salmon in this recipe. How do you know the difference? Cold-smoked salmon still looks raw and hot-smoked looks cooked. They're roughly the same price, so try them both out and see which you prefer.

　Butter for the pan

1　large yellow onion, diced

1　pound potatoes (reds or Yukon golds will work), peeled and diced

8　ounces hot- or cold-smoked salmon

1　cup asparagus, roughly chopped

Tangy Dill Vinaigrette (below)

1 In a large sauté pan (that you have a lid for), melt a few tablespoons of butter over medium heat. Add onion and potatoes. Place the lid over the pan. Peek in and stir occasionally, allowing the onions and potatoes to cook through until tender enough that a fork pierces the potato.

2 Add smoked salmon, asparagus, and a tad more butter and simmer uncovered. Stir occasionally and let the mixture develop a crispy crust—about 10 more minutes should do it.

3 Toss the hash with Tangy Dill Vinaigrette.

TANGY DILL VINAIGRETTE

MAKES ABOUT ½ CUP

1　tablespoon fresh dill, minced

1　tablespoon Dijon mustard

3　tablespoons extra virgin olive oil

2　tablespoons lemon juice

2　teaspoons prepared horseradish

Salt and pepper to taste

1 Place all ingredients in a small bowl and whisk to combine.

2 Store in the fridge for up to 1 week.

BACON TEN WAYS

SERVES 2 TO 4

On its own, bacon is pretty spectacular, but by adding sweet, spicy, and salty flavorings to it, you can make it unimaginably amazing. The only problem is choosing which flavors you want to try. Spread or sprinkle on one of each flavor to create a flavored-bacon sampler.

1 pound sliced bacon

Barbecue sauce

Sriracha or chili garlic sauce

Mango chutney

100 percent fruit strawberry jam

Applesauce and cinnamon

Maple syrup and black pepper

Dijon mustard

Curry powder

Old Bay seasoning

Country Breakfast Sausage seasoning (page 264)

1 Preheat oven to 350°F.

2 Lay bacon on a baking sheet.

3 Choose your flavor(s). Use a spoon to spread sauces (not too thick), and use your fingers to sprinkle spice blends on top of each slice.

4 Bake until the bacon is evenly browned and crisp, about 25 minutes.

MEATS & MAINS

COCONUT SHRIMP CAKES
SERVES 6

1   cup unsweetened coconut, shredded

1   egg

1   pound cod filets

1   pound shrimp, peeled and deveined

Salt to taste

Coconut oil

Pineapple Salsa (below)

1 Place shredded coconut in a bowl.

2 Blend egg, cod, shrimp, and salt in a food processor until relatively smooth.

3 Use your hand or a scoop to form the seafood mixture into balls about 2 inches in diameter. Pat them into disc shapes, and coat them in shredded coconut.

4 In a large skillet, melt coconut oil over medium heat.

5 Fry the cakes until golden brown, about 3 to 4 minutes per side.

6 Serve with Pineapple Salsa.

PINEAPPLE SALSA

½   pineapple, cut into small chunks

2   tablespoons fresh cilantro

1   tablespoon apple cider vinegar

Juice of 1 lime

Salt to taste

1 Purée all ingredients in a food processor until smooth.

2 Alternatively, you can make the salsa a bit more chucky and roughly chop everything with a knife.

CRAWFISH ÉTOUFFÉE

SERVES 6

Looks tasty and tastes even tastier. Serve with Root Risotto (page 178).

- 6 ounces bacon, chopped
- 2 celery stalks, chopped
- 1 green bell pepper, chopped
- 1 yellow onion, chopped
- 2 tablespoons potato flour
- 2 cups chicken stock
- ½ 14.5-ounce can crushed tomatoes
- 1 pound crawfish tail meat
- 2 tablespoons Worcestershire sauce
- 2 tablespoons hot sauce
- 2 bay leaves, torn in half
- 1 tablespoon lemon juice
- 1 tablespoon fresh thyme, minced
- Salt and pepper to taste

1 In a high-sided sauté pan, brown the bacon over medium heat. Remove from pan and set aside.

2 Add in celery, bell pepper, and onion. Cook until soft, about 5 minutes.

3 Whisk in potato flour and sauté for 1 minute. Whisk in chicken stock, tomatoes, crawfish, Worcestershire sauce, hot sauce, bay leaf, lemon juice, and thyme. Season with salt and pepper. Bring to a simmer and cook for 8 to 10 minutes, until bubbly and thickened.

4 From here, you can either stir the bacon into the mix, or use it as a garnish when serving.

5 Remove bay leaves before serving.

SEAFOOD POT PIE WITH CHEDDAR CRUMBLE BISCUIT

SERVES 6

It's like clam chowder meets chicken pot pie. We can think of no better winter comfort food. If you don't eat cheese, make the Biscuit recipe on page 56 as a substitute.

FOR THE FILLING

    Butter for the pan

3 celery stalks, diced

2 leeks, chopped

½ shallot, minced

½ cup chicken (or seafood) stock

¼ cup heavy cream

1 tablespoon tapioca flour

¼ pound shrimp, peeled and deveined

1 6.5-ounce can clams in juice

1 pound cod filets, cut into chunks

¼ pound bay scallops

    Salt to taste

FOR THE BISCUIT TOPPING

⅓ cup tapioca flour

⅓ cup coconut flour

2 teaspoons baking soda

2 green onions, chopped

8 ounces shredded cheddar cheese

½ cup water

1 Preheat oven to 350°F.

2 In a large soup pot, sauté celery, leeks, and shallot in butter over medium-high heat. Stir in chicken stock, cream, tapioca flour, and seafood.

3 Place the heat on medium, and allow the seafood to cook through. Then flake the cod into bite-sized chunks.

4 In a large bowl, combine tapioca and coconut flours, baking soda, green onions, and cheddar cheese. Add the water one tablespoon at a time until crumbs start to form.

5 Spoon the seafood filling into a large oven-safe baking dish. Pour the biscuit crumbs on top evenly over the entire dish.

6 Bake until golden brown and bubbly, about 30 minutes.

PASTRAMI SALMON

SERVES 6

Salmon is most persnickety when it comes to how it likes to be cooked. Overcook it and you'll find yourself chowing down on a close approximation of cat food. So we'll toss it in a pastrami bath and you'll never have to feast on cat food again.

- 2   quarts water
- ¼   cup coconut sugar
- ¼   cup salt
- 1   tablespoon powdered ginger
- 1   tablespoon ground coriander
- 1   tablespoon juniper berries
- 2   cinnamon sticks
- 2   bay leaves, torn into pieces
- 1   teaspoon black peppercorns
- 1   teaspoon brown mustard seeds
- 4   garlic cloves, peeled and crushed
- 2   pounds salmon, skinned and picked over for pin bones

Oil for the pan

1 In a large pot, bring water, coconut sugar, and salt to a simmer. Stir occasionally until salt and sugar are dissolved.

2 To a small sauté pan, add ginger, coriander, juniper berries, cinnamon sticks, bay leaves, peppercorns, and mustard seeds. Heat over medium-low and toss the spices around until you start to hear them snap, crackle, and pop. Remove from heat and stir the spices into the hot sugar-salt solution. Add the garlic. Let the brine cool to room temperature.

3 Transfer the brine to a large container or bowl, then add the salmon. Cover the container with a lid or plastic wrap and place in the refrigerator. Allow the salmon to marinate for at least 24 hours, but no more than 48 hours or the salmon will be too salty.

4 After marinating, remove salmon from brine and pat dry with paper towels. Discard the brine.

5 In a large sauté pan, melt a tablespoon of oil over medium heat. Sear the salmon until a crust forms on the outside. Do not over sear. The inside of the fish should be very slightly underdone. Depending on the thickness of your salmon, sear about 3 minutes per side.

6 Serve with sauerkraut and a good mustard.

SHRIMP PAD THAI

SERVES 4

Cutting zucchini into noodle shapes (aka zoodles), is a bit on the tedious side, so another option for speed, lack of the proper tools, or sheer laziness is to just chop the zucchini into chunks. Not quite the same effect, but it will have the same flavor. Make this more budget friendly by using chicken thighs or breasts instead of shrimp.

Butter for the pan

1½ pounds shrimp

1 pound zucchini

1 onion, diced

4 garlic cloves, minced

1 tablespoon fresh, minced ginger

1 tablespoon apple cider vinegar

3 tablespoons almond butter

1 teaspoon Sriracha or chili garlic sauce

1 teaspoon fish sauce

2 tablespoons lime juice

Salt to taste

1 With a mandoline, slice the zucchinis lengthwise into thin planks. Then with a knife, slice the planks into thin strips that resemble spaghetti. Alternatively, you can also use a julienne peeler or a knife to slice the zukes as thinly as you can.

2 Over medium heat, melt a tablespoon of butter. Add the shrimp and sauté until pink. Remove shrimp from the pan and set aside.

3 In same pan, melt more butter if needed, and sauté the onion, garlic, and ginger, until soft. Add the vinegar, almond butter, chili garlic sauce, fish sauce, lime juice, and salt. Stir to combine.

4 Add the zucchini noodles to the sauté pan. Stir them around to get the sauce onto the "zoodles." The point here is get the zoodles hot and very slightly cooked through (just like an al dente noodle!), about 5 minutes.

5 Add the shrimp back to the pan. Stir to combine and serve immediately.

GYRO TACO SALAD & TZATZIKI GUACAMOLE

SERVES 6

FOR THE GYRO TACO SALAD

- 2 pounds ground lamb
- 1 large yellow onion, diced
- 4 garlic cloves, minced
- 1 teaspoon dried oregano
- 1 teaspoon dried thyme
- 1 teaspoon ground coriander
- ½ cup chicken stock
- 1 tablespoon lemon juice
- Salt to taste
- 3 heads romaine lettuce

1 In a large sauté pan, brown the lamb. Once the lamb looks about halfway cooked through, add the onion and garlic. Continue to cook until onion is softened. Add the oregano, thyme, coriander, chicken stock, lemon juice, and salt. Cook about 5 minutes more, until the stock has reduced a bit.

2 Chop the romaine lettuce and serve with gyro meat and a spoonful of tzatziki guacamole.

FOR THE TZATZIKI GUACAMOLE

- 2 ripe Haas avocados
- 1 English cucumber
- 1 tablespoon fresh mint
- 1 tablespoon fresh dill
- 1 tablespoon lemon juice
- Salt to taste

1 Shred the cucumber with a box grater over a tea towel.

2 Twist the tea towel up, and squeeze it over the kitchen sink to remove excess water from cucumber.

3 Blend avocados, squeezed cucumber, mint, dill, lemon, and salt in a food processor until smooth.

SPANAKOPITA SOUP

SERVES 4

Italian wedding soup meets a big, fat Greek wedding...soup.

FOR THE MEATBALLS

- 1   pound ground lamb
- 2   tablespoons fresh dill, minced
- 1   10-ounce package frozen spinach, thawed
- 1   egg
- 1   tablespoon lemon zest
- ¼   teaspoon grated nutmeg

   Salt to taste

FOR THE SOUP

   Butter for the pan
- 2   stalks celery, diced
- ½   yellow onion, chopped
- 3   garlic cloves, minced
- 1   quart chicken stock
- 2   tablespoons lemon juice

   Feta cheese (optional)

1 Over medium heat, melt about 2 tablespoons of butter in a large soup pot. Add celery, onion, and garlic. Sauté until soft. Add chicken stock and lemon juice. Bring to a simmer.

2 Meanwhile, in a large bowl, mix together ground lamb, dill, spinach, egg, lemon zest, nutmeg, and salt. Form mixture into bite-size meatballs. Place meatballs into the simmering chicken stock, and continue to simmer until the meatballs are cooked through, about 5 minutes.

3 Optionally, serve with feta cheese crumbled on top.

MOO SHU CABBAGE CUPS

SERVES 6

Get dinner on the table in less than 30 minutes. Not fast enough? Make this dish truly light speed by substituting 1 teaspoon onion powder, 1 teaspoon granulated garlic, and 1 teaspoon powdered ginger for fresh.

1	Napa cabbage
2	pounds ground pork
1	large yellow onion, diced
8	ounces mushrooms, sliced
1	tablespoon fresh garlic, minced
1	tablespoon fresh ginger, minced
¼	cup reduced-sodium, wheat-free, soy sauce (or coconut aminos)
1	tablespoon apple cider vinegar
1	tablespoon sesame oil
2	green onions, finely chopped

1 Cut the end off of the cabbage and discard. Remove any damaged leaves. Set aside the larger leaves, and chop the cabbage leaves that are too small to use as cups.

2 In a large skillet, brown the pork and remove from pan.

3 In the same pan, sauté the onion, mushrooms, chopped cabbage, garlic, and ginger until soft.

4 Stir in soy sauce, vinegar, and sesame oil. Add the pork back to the pan and stir to combine.

5 Fill reserved cabbage leaves with the pork mixture. Garnish with green onion and serve.

BEST-EVER PULLED PORK

SERVES 8

This meat is so flavorful on its own that saucing it with anything other than the broth it cooked in is totally unnecessary. But if you really want to change it up, try tossing the meat together with Chimichurri Sauce (page 164).

4   pounds pork butt

Salt and pepper to taste

Extra virgin olive oil for the pan

6   garlic cloves, peeled and smashed

1   yellow onion, roughly chopped

2   teaspoons cumin seeds

3   bay leaves, torn in half

1   quart chicken stock

1 Preheat oven to 300°F.

2 Generously salt and pepper the pork.

3 In a large dutch oven, heat a few tablespoons of olive oil over medium-high heat. Sear pork on all sides until a brown crust forms. Remove from the pan and set aside.

4 Add garlic, onions, cumin seeds, and bay leaves. Sauté until the onions are soft.

5 Add chicken stock to the pan, scraping up any brown bits that have attached themselves to the bottom of the pan. Add the pork.

6 Cover with lid slightly ajar and roast for 4 hours. Remove lid and roast for an additional hour.

7 Remove from the oven and allow to cool. Use two forks (or your hands) to pull the pork into chunks.

CUBAN BURGER

SERVES 6

These might be fightin' words, but we'd venture to say this is better than any Cuban sandwich we've had on the streets of Miami.

FOR THE "BUN"

3 green plantains

Coconut oil

Salt to taste

FOR THE BURGER

2 pounds ground pork

1 tablespoon onion powder

1 tablespoon dried oregano

2 teaspoons granulated garlic

1 tablespoon lime juice

Salt to taste

FOR THE TOPPINGS

Shaved deli ham

Yellow mustard

Honey

Dill pickles

1 For the buns, peel the plantains and slice into 2-inch-thick rounds.

2 Bring a large pot of water to a boil. Boil plantain rounds until soft, about 5 minutes.

3 Remove the plantains and smash flat with the back of a plate. If the plantain sticks to the plate, scrape it off with a spatula. Season with salt.

4 In a skillet, melt a few tablespoons of coconut oil over medium-high heat. Fry flattened plantains until brown and crispy, about 3 minutes per side.

5 For the burger, place all ingredients in a bowl. Use your hands to mix everything together thoroughly. Form the burgers roughly the same size as the plantain buns.

6 Cook the burgers in the skillet, adding more oil if needed, about 5 minutes per side.

7 To assemble, place a bun on a plate, top with a burger patty, plus any desired toppings, and cap off with another plantain bun.

8 Serve immediately.

SPAGHETTI SQUASH CARBONARA

Spaghetti squash is typically used as a low-carb, grain-free substitute for pasta. So, with this recipe, we're thinking outside the pasta box.

FOR THE FILLING

1	3-pound spaghetti squash
1	pound bacon, sliced into strips
4	ounces finely grated Parmesan cheese
¼	teaspoon nutmeg
½	teaspoon ground black pepper

1 Preheat oven to 400°F.

2 Place the spaghetti squash on a baking sheet and put in the oven. Unless you want to risk the chance of cutting off a finger or two, we aren't cutting the squash in half first; stick it in there whole. Roast until the squash skin is soft and caves in a bit when you poke it, about 30 minutes.

3 Meanwhile, in a large skillet, sauté the bacon until crispy. When done, remove bacon from the skillet, and let it drain on a plate lined with paper towels.

4 Once the squash is cool to the touch, use a knife to split it in half lengthwise. Remove the seeds with a spoon. Scoop the flesh out into a large bowl.

5 Add nutmeg, black pepper, and Parmesan cheese (save some for garnish). Mix to combine.

6 Serve with crispy bacon and a little extra Parmesan on top.

BALSAMIC & ARUGULA PIZZA WITH PROSCIUTTO

MAKES ONE 14-INCH PIZZA

1	Pizza Crust (page 259), prebaked
½	large red onion, thinly sliced
¼	cup balsamic vinegar
1	cup Pizza Sauce (page 263 or store-bought)
2	ounces prosciutto, thinly sliced
2	ounces goat cheese (optional)
1	cup provolone or mozzarella, grated (optional)
2	handfuls arugula
	Extra virgin olive oil
	Salt to taste

1 Prepare and prebake Pizza Crust (page 259).

2 In a large sauté pan, heat a tablespoon of olive oil over medium-low heat. Add sliced onion. Stir occasionally, until the onions have softened. Add balsamic vinegar and cook until all the liquid is absorbed into the onions.

3 Top prebaked crust with sauce, cheese, prosciutto, and onions. Broil on high until the cheese has melted, about 3 to 4 minutes. Add arugula and a few splashes of olive oil.

BUTTERNUT SQUASH LASAGNA

SERVES 4 TO 6

Look for a long squash when shopping, as it'll be infinitely easier to cut up. You'll use just the shaft for this recipe, but can save the bulbous parts for another dish like the Roasted Squash and Beet Salad on page 161.

1	pound Hot Italian Sausage (page 265 or store-bought)
1	red onion, chopped
3	garlic cloves, minced
2	cups Pizza Sauce (page 263 or store-bought)
½	cup roasted red peppers (about 1 whole)
¼	cup extra virgin olive oil
2	tablespoons fresh basil, chopped
1	large, long butternut squash
1	cup mozzarella cheese (optional)

1 Preheat oven to 400°F.

2 In a sauté pan, crumble the sausage and add the onion and garlic. Cook until sausage is browned.

3 Meanwhile, slice off the ends of the squash. Next, cut the bulbous part off, leaving a long shaft that should be at least 4 inches long. Peel the squash. Using a mandoline, slice the shaft into thin slices and set aside. As it's a bit harder to cut the bulbous part (where all the seeds and stringy bits are) into uniform pieces, save it to use later for another dish.

4 Make the sauce by puréeing pizza sauce, red peppers, olive oil, and basil. If you don't have a contraption that will purée (blender, food processor, immersion blender), chop up the red peppers and just whisk everything together.

5 In an 8 x 10 x 3-inch baking dish, spoon down enough sauce to lightly cover the bottom of the dish. (This keeps the squash from sticking to the pan.) Next add the squash, then spoon on the sausage mixture, followed by the sauce. Repeat until all the ingredients are used. Save enough sauce to cover the top of the lasagna.

6 Bake for 1 hour. You're looking for a bubbly pan with a crispy, browned top. Right out of the oven, the lasagna may be liquidy, so let it set for a good half-hour before cutting into it.

LOADED FAUXTATO SOUP

1	large head of cauliflower
3	garlic cloves, crushed
1	quart chicken stock
1	tablespoon lemon juice
	Salt to taste

TOPPINGS

Crispy bacon

Sliced green onions

Butter

1 Cut cauliflower in half, lengthwise. Cut out the core and remove the outer green leaves. Roughly chop the cauliflower into pieces.

2 Add cauliflower pieces, garlic, chicken stock, and lemon juice to a large soup pot. Bring to a boil, then turn down to simmer. Continue to cook until the cauliflower is tender.

3 Meanwhile, if you're using bacon, now is the time to cook it. Chop it into strips and sauté over medium heat until crispy.

4 Transfer the cauliflower mixture to a blender and blend until smooth.

5 Top soup with crispy bacon, green onions, and a pat of butter.

CHORIZO STUFFED PORK CHOPS

SERVES 4

Cut into this thick, juicy pork chop, and SURPRISE...more pork!

Butter for the pan

½ pound fresh Chorizo (page 266 or store-bought)

1 sweet potato, peeled and cut into ¼-inch cubes

4 green onions, diced

4 thick-cut, bone-in pork chops at least 1-inch thick

Salt and pepper to taste

1 Preheat oven to 350°F.

2 Heat a sauté pan over medium heat. Melt a tablespoon of butter, add the chorizo, and brown for about 5 minutes, until cooked through. Remove chorizo from the pan and set aside, leaving drippings. In the same pan, sauté sweet potatoes for 5 minutes until soft and combine with the cooked chorizo and diced green onions. Now you're ready for stuffin'.

3 Using a small knife, cut a slit into the fatty side of each pork chop. Be careful not to slice clear through and separate the chop into two pieces. The idea here is to create a pouch. Think "coin purse." The bigger you can make the stuffing cavity with a small opening, the better your stuffing will stay in and the more goodies you can fit into your chops. Once the pouches are cut, season both sides of the pork chops liberally with salt and pepper.

4 Pack the chops with as much of the sweet potato-chorizo mixture as you can fit, and secure with a toothpick if necessary. Save the leftover chorizo for a nice snack.

5 Melt 2 tablespoons of butter in a sauté pan. Over high heat, sear the chops for 3 to 5 minutes on each side until browned. Then pop 'em in the oven for another 10 to 12 minutes, until the pork chops reach an internal temperature of 160°F on a meat thermometer.

BACON LATTICE & TOMATO SANDWICH

MAKES 2 SANDWICHES

A woven blanket of bacony goodness, spread with a dollop of roasted garlic mayonnaise and a few fresh veggies to make your mom happy.

FOR THE BACON LATTICE SANDWICH

12 slices bacon

1 large ripe tomato, sliced

1 cup arugula or other crunchy lettuce

Black pepper to taste

1 Preheat oven to 400°F.

2 To make the bacon lattice, lay 6 strips of bacon side-by-side on a baking sheet, with no gaps in between.

3 Fold the first, third, and fifth strip halfway back; then, at the folds, place a new strip of bacon perpendicular to the first ones.

4 Return the folded strips so they overlap the new strip. Fold back the second, fourth and sixth strips; arrange another perpendicular strip at the folds.

5 Repeat steps 3 and 4 until a lattice is formed. Season with pepper, if you'd like.

6 Bake until crisp, about 40 minutes. Cut the lattice into fourths.

7 To assemble the sandwiches, smear some roasted garlic mayonnaise onto a bacon lattice. Top with tomato slices, a small handful of arugula, and another lattice piece.

FOR THE ROASTED GARLIC MAYONNAISE

6 garlic cloves

Extra virgin olive oil

mayonnaise (page 262)

Salt to taste

1 Preheat oven to 300°F.

2 Rip off a square piece of aluminum foil and place garlic cloves and a few glugs of olive oil inside. Scrunch up the foil into a loose ball, and pop it in the oven until the garlic is golden brown, about 20 minutes.

3 Add mayonnaise to your food processor. Pop the roasted garlic cloves out of their jackets and stick in the food processor. Buzz to incorporate. Add salt to taste.

4 Save the leftovers to enjoy later.

CHICKEN ENCHILADA EMPANADAS

MAKES 10 EMPANADAS

FOR THE FILLING

- 1   15-ounce can tomato sauce
- ½   cup chicken stock
- 1   tablespoon chili powder
- 2   teaspoons paprika
- 2   teaspoons granulated garlic
- 1   teaspoon smoked paprika
- 1   teaspoon powdered onion
- 1   teaspoon ground coriander
- Salt to taste
- 1   pound chicken breast, cut into small cubes
- 4   ounces goat cheese (optional)

FOR THE DOUGH

- 2   cups tapioca flour
- ½   cup potato flour
- 2   teaspoons salt
- ¾   cup water
- 2   teaspoons powdered gelatin
- ½   cup high oleic sunflower oil
- 2   eggs

FOR THE EGG WASH

- 1   egg yolk
- 1   tablespoon water

1 Preheat oven to 400°F. Lightly grease a sheet pan.

2 In a sauce pot, combine tomato sauce, chicken stock, and spices. Add cubed chicken breast and bring to a simmer. Continue to simmer for 20 minutes.

3 Meanwhile, prepare the dough. Combine flours and salt in a large bowl. Add water to another large bowl and sprinkle in gelatin. Let sit for 1 minute. Whisk in oil and eggs. Whisk wet ingredients into dry, and knead until a dough has formed.

4 Divide the dough into 10 uniform balls. Split each ball in half. Use your hands to press the dough into very thin discs. Place one disc on the sheet pan, top with 3 tablespoons of enchilada filling and goat cheese (if using). Top with another dough disc. Roll the sides of the dough up around the filling and press to create a seal. Continue until all the dough has been used.

5 Use a pastry brush to lightly brush the empanadas with egg wash.

6 Bake until golden brown, about 28 to 30 minutes.

SWEET & SOUR SPLIT ROAST CHICKEN

SERVES 2 TO 4

Roasted chicken is a comfort meal that speaks to all regions of the US—definitely an important recipe that every cook should have in his or her repertoire. Not only is it an economical way to feed the family, but it also pulls double duty: there are countless ways to season and eat the meat, AND you can save the bones to make stock.

1   5-pound fryer chicken, giblets removed

Salt

FOR SWEET & SOUR SAUCE

½   cup pineapple juice

1   tablespoon 100 percent fruit apricot jam

1   tablespoon wheat-free, reduced sodium soy sauce or coconut aminos

1   tablespoon ketchup

3   tablespoons apple cider vinegar

½   teaspoon powdered ginger

1 For the moistest roasted chicken ever created, it's ultra super important to bring the chicken to room temperature. If you stick the chicken in the oven straight out of the refrigerator, a lot of the cooking time is spent trying to bring the temperature of the chicken up—and by doing it this way, you're getting different temperatures within different parts of the chicken, so some parts cook faster than others, resulting in dry chicken. Anyway…

2 Preheat oven to 400°F.

3 Now split the chicken in half—another trick that will help the chicken cook faster and keep it moist. Using a pair of kitchen shears (or a cleaver), cut the chicken along its back (not the breast side), making sure you start cutting to the side of the backbone and not on the actual backbone. Sit the chicken on the counter to give yourself a sturdy base and start at the neck opening, cutting down towards the end at the tailbone. The chicken will look like it's doing a split—sort of. Discard the backbone or save it to make chicken stock. Lay the chicken, breast side up, in a roasting pan or large baking dish. Sprinkle the chicken with salt and let it hang out while it comes up to room temperature.

4 In a sauce pot, over medium heat, whisk together pineapple juice, jam, soy sauce, ketchup, vinegar, and ginger, until the sauce comes together.

5 Clean off the underside of a cast-iron pan and lightly grease it with oil. Put the chicken in the oven and place the bottom of the pan on top of the chicken. This allows the oven heat to cook the chicken from the bottom while the cast-iron pan crisps the bird from the top. Bake until the temperature in the thigh of the chicken is around 150°F to 165°F. It should take about 45 minutes. When done, carefully remove the cast-iron pan from the chicken.

6 Brush on the sweet and sour sauce. Turn the oven on to broil and peek at the chicken every minute until it's crispy and done to your liking.

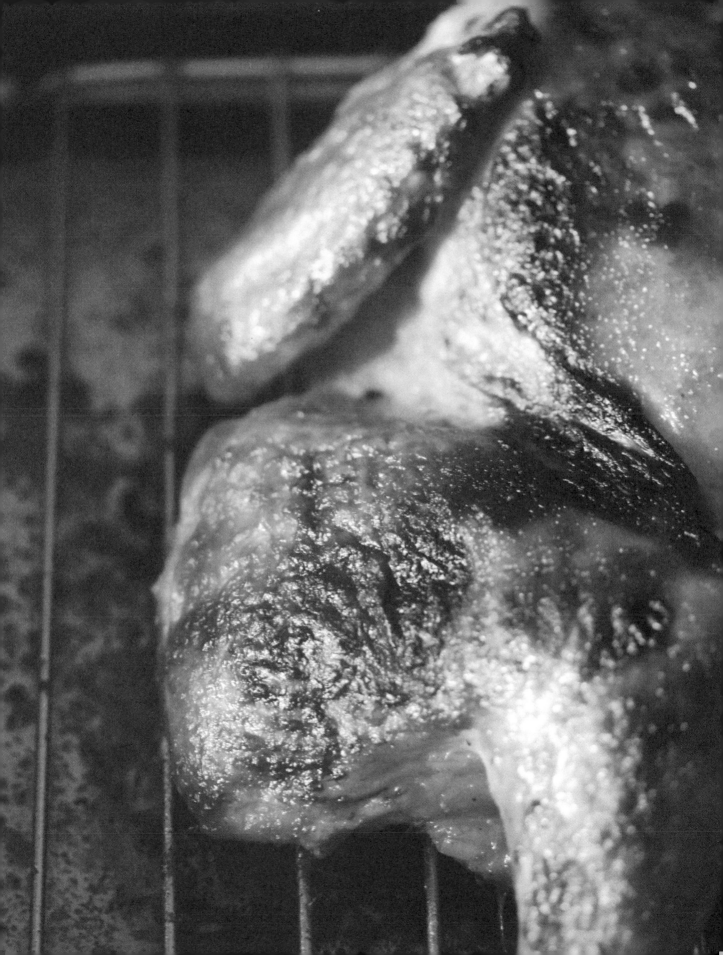

CRISPY CHICKEN FINGERS

SERVES 6

On the "Favorite Food" list of almost every child I know (and some adults, too). For an Asian-inspired dipping sauce, make the sauce featured in the Sweet & Sour Split Roast Chicken recipe (page 110).

½ cup palm shortening

2 pounds chicken tenderloins or chicken breast cut into strips

1 cup tapioca flour

1 teaspoon onion powder

½ teaspoon granulated garlic

¼ teaspoon cayenne pepper

½ teaspoon salt

2 eggs

1 tablespoon water

1 Whisk together tapioca flour, onion, garlic, cayenne, and salt in a large bowl.

2 In a separate bowl, whisk together eggs and water.

3 In a large skillet, melt palm shortening over medium heat.

4 Dip chicken one piece at a time in egg mixture, then coat in the tapioca flour mixture.

5 Lay chicken in the skillet and fry until both sides are slightly brown and crispy, about 3 to 5 minutes per side.

6 Serve immediately.

THAI CHILI CHICKEN MEATBALLS

SERVES 6 TO 8

FOR THE MEATBALLS

- 2 pounds ground chicken (ground turkey will work well, too.)
- 2 tablespoons coconut flour
- 2 tablespoons fresh cilantro, chopped
- 2 eggs
- 2 tablespoons 100 percent fruit peach jam
- ½ teaspoon chili garlic sauce

Salt to taste

FOR THE THAI CHILI SAUCE

- ½ cup 100 percent fruit peach jam
- ½ cup apple cider vinegar
- 1 teaspoon chili garlic sauce
- 2 tablespoons water
- 2 tablespoons fresh cilantro, chopped

1 Preheat oven to 400°F. Line a baking sheet with parchment paper or use a silicone pat.

2 In a large bowl, use your hands to mix together the meatball ingredients.

3 Using your hand or a scoop, form balls roughly 1½-inches in diameter and place on the baking sheet. Bake for 20 to 25 minutes.

4 Meanwhile, combine the chili sauce ingredients in a sauté pan. Cook over medium-high heat until the sauce starts to bubble.

5 Place the chili sauce in a large bowl. Once the meatballs are cooked through, add them to the bowl of sauce and toss gently to coat.

HOT & SOUR CHICKEN NOODLE SOUP

SERVES 4 TO 6

Shirataki noodles are traditional Japanese noodles made from the Konjac plant. With almost no nutritive content, they don't have much of a taste, but are the best gluten- and grain-free noodle substitute we've tasted (We aren't fans of kelp noodles, but they work well as a substitute). We use Miracle Noodle brand, which you can find in some natural and whole food grocery stores and online.

2   pounds boneless, skinless chicken thighs

Palm shortening for the pan

3   carrots, peeled and chopped

1   tablespoon fresh ginger, minced

3   garlic cloves, minced

6   ounces shiitake mushrooms, sliced, stems removed

1   quart chicken stock

¼   cup apple cider vinegar

1   tablespoon wheat-free, reduced sodium soy sauce or coconut aminos

2   teaspoons chili garlic sauce (or your favorite hot sauce)

2   7-ounce packages Shirataki fettuccine noodles

Fresh cilantro for garnish

1 Chop chicken thighs into small chunks.

2 Melt a few tablespoons of palm shortening in a large soup pot over medium-high heat. Add chicken and cook until browned.

3 Add carrots, ginger, garlic, and mushrooms to the pot. Sauté until softened.

4 Add chicken stock, apple cider vinegar, soy sauce, and chili garlic sauce. Stir to combine.

5 Rinse off noodles according to package instructions. They're a bit too long straight out of the package, so cut them down with a knife before adding to the pot.

6 Top with fresh cilantro and serve.

TIKKA MASALA CHICKEN WINGS

SERVES 6

FOR THE WINGS

3 pounds chicken wings

Extra virgin olive oil for the pan

FOR THE TIKKA MASALA SAUCE

1 teaspoon garam masala

1 teaspoon powdered ginger

1 teaspoon ground coriander

1 teaspoon ground cumin

1 teaspoon ground cardamom

½ teaspoon granulated garlic

¼ teaspoon cayenne pepper

Salt to taste

2 tablespoons tomato paste

½ cup coconut milk

1 Preheat oven to 400°F. Place the oven rack in the middle of the oven.

2 Lightly grease a baking sheet with olive oil. Place chicken wings skin-side down on the baking sheet and bake for 15 minutes.

3 Using tongs, flip the wings over to skin-side up, and turn the oven to broil. Broil until the skin is crispy, about another 15 minutes.

4 Meanwhile, make the sauce. Combine spices in a medium sauté pan. With the heat on low, sauté the spices until fragrant, about 5 minutes. Whisk in tomato paste and coconut milk.

5 Once the wings are crispy and out of the oven, toss them in the masala sauce.

CURRY TURKEY BURGERS & MANGO SLAW

SERVES 6

Because there's no need to sit by the skillet and individually pan-fry these, you can have a flavorful, elegant meal on the table in less than 30 minutes.

FOR THE BURGERS

- 2 pounds ground turkey
- 1 tablespoon red curry paste
- 3 green onions, minced
- Salt to taste

FOR THE MANGO SLAW

- 2 ripe mangoes, peeled and pitted
- 2 red bell peppers
- 1 English cucumber
- 3 green onions, minced
- 1 teaspoon lime zest
- 2 tablespoons lime juice
- 1 teaspoon honey
- 2 tablespoons fresh mint leaves, minced
- ½ teaspoon red curry paste
- Salt to taste

1 Preheat oven to 400°F. Line a baking sheet with aluminum foil, and top with the rack from a roasting pan.

2 In a large bowl, combine turkey, curry paste, green onions, and salt.

3 Shape meat into patties and place on the roasting rack. Bake the patties until the burgers are cooked through, about 20 minutes.

4 Prepare the slaw while the burgers are cooking.

1 Cut mangoes, peppers, cucumbers, and onions into thin strips and place in a large serving bowl. Stir in lime zest, lime juice, honey, mint, curry paste, and salt.

2 Let marinate in the fridge for at least 15 minutes.

BUFFALO CHICKEN SALAD

SERVES 4

All the goodness of wings and celery, without the sticky fingers. This a great portable option when you've got a hankering for chicken wings.

1½   pounds chicken breast

2   celery stalks, chopped, plus 1 cup, diced

½   yellow onion, chopped

½   cup mayonnaise (page 262)

¼   cup hot sauce

Salt to taste

1 Place chicken breasts in a pot. Add enough water to cover the chicken. Add chopped celery with the onion and salt. Bring to a simmer and cook for 10 minutes.

2 Turn off the heat and allow the chicken to continue to cook for 10 to 15 more minutes in the hot water. Check to ensure chicken is cooked through and shred when cool enough to handle.

3 In a mixing bowl add mayonnaise, hot sauce, diced celery, and shredded chicken. Mix to combine.

CHILI PIE

SERVES 6

3   green plantains

3   tablespoons palm shortening, melted

¼   teaspoon granulated garlic

¼   teaspoon ground cumin

½   teaspoon chili powder

¼   teaspoon cayenne pepper

Salt to taste

FOR THE CHILI

Butter for the pan

1   yellow onion, diced

2   pounds ground beef

2   cups tomato sauce

1   4-ounce can diced green chilies

2   tablespoons chili powder

2   teaspoons ground cumin

2   teaspoons granulated garlic

¼   teaspoon cayenne pepper

¼   cup pickled jalapeños

Salt to taste

1 Preheat oven to 350°F. Peel the plantains and cut them in half lengthwise, then split them into quarters.

2 Using a mandoline, place the plantains flat (cut side down), and slice approximately ⅛-inch thick.

3 In a large bowl, mix together the garlic, cumin, chili powder, cayenne, and salt. Add the melted palm shortening.

4 Add the plantain strips to the oil and spices. Some will stick together; take the time to separate them and make sure both sides get coated.

5 On a baking sheet, place plantains in one layer, with no overlap. This usually takes 2 baking sheets. Bake 15 to 17 minutes, until golden brown around the edges. If you have baking sheets on 2 oven racks, keep an eye on them as you may need to swap the pans halfway through baking for even cooking.

6 Meanwhile, make the chili. In a large pot, melt a tablespoon of butter over medium heat. Add half the onion (setting aside the other half for garnish) and cook until translucent. Add beef and brown. Except the jalapeños, add the rest of the ingredients, and simmer while the plantain chips bake in the oven, about 20 minutes.

7 Top with reserved diced onion and pickled jalapeños.

ITALIAN FAJITAS & BRUSCHETTA SALSA

SERVES 4

Standard Mexican restaurant fare meets Italian flavors.

FOR THE FAJITAS

Butter for the pan

1 pound skirt steak, cut into thin strips

3 garlic cloves, minced

2 teaspoons Italian seasoning blend

2 bell peppers, cut into strips

1 yellow onion, cut into strips

Salt and pepper to taste

FOR THE BRUSCHETTA SALSA

1 pound tomatoes, diced

1 yellow onion, diced

Handful of fresh basil leaves, chopped

2 tablespoons extra virgin olive oil

2 tablespoons balsamic vinegar

Salt to taste

1 In a large skillet, heat about a tablespoon of butter over high heat. Season steak strips with salt, pepper, and Italian seasoning. Add steak strips to skillet and sauté until browned, about 5 minutes. Once cooked, remove steak strips from pan and set aside.

2 Reduce the heat to medium. Add the garlic, bell pepper strips, and onion. Cover with a lid and cook for another 5 to 8 minutes, stirring occasionally until vegetables are soft.

3 Meanwhile, in a large bowl, add the salsa ingredients together and stir to combine.

4 Top fajitas with bruschetta and serve.

PUMPKIN CHILI & ZESTY GUACAMOLE

SERVES 6 TO 8

Don't overlook this recipe simply because of the long list of ingredients. This chili comes together with a super short prep and cook time. Top with a plop of one the most uniquely flavored guacamoles you've ever tasted, and you've got a chili recipe that will definitely make its way into your weekly meal rotation.

FOR THE CHILI

2   pounds ground beef

1   yellow onion, diced

3   garlic cloves, minced

½   cup pumpkin purée

1   28-ounce can crushed tomatoes

1   15-ounce can tomato sauce

1   4-ounce can diced green chilis

1   cup beef stock

2   tablespoons chili powder

1   tablespoon ground cumin

1   tablespoon paprika

2   teaspoons ground coriander

2   teaspoons cinnamon

2   teaspoons cocoa powder

1   teaspoon granulated garlic

¼   teaspoon cayenne pepper

Salt to taste

FOR THE GUACAMOLE

3   ripe Haas avocados

2   teaspoons ground coriander

1   teaspoon orange zest

2   tablespoons orange juice

2   tablespoons lime juice

Salt to taste

1 In a large soup pot, place beef, onion, and garlic over medium heat, stirring occasionally until the beef is browned.

2 Add the rest of the chili ingredients. Let simmer, stirring every so often for 15 minutes.

3 Meanwhile, make the guacamole. In a food processor, buzz together all the ingredients. If you don't have a food processor, you can place all the ingredients in a bowl, and use a fork to mash everything together.

PHILLY STUFFED PEPPERS

SERVES 4 TO 6

If you're trying to stay on a budget, stick to using green bell peppers.

2 yellow onions, thinly sliced

8 ounces mushrooms, sliced

1 pound ground beef

2 tablespoons hot sauce

3 tablespoons Worcestershire sauce

4 bell peppers

4 ounces provolone cheese (optional)

Butter for the pan

1 Preheat oven to 350°F.

2 Cut each pepper in half lengthwise. Remove stems and pick out the white membrane and seeds. Place peppers on a baking tray and bake until tender, about 15 minutes.

3 Meanwhile, in a large sauté pan, melt a tablespoon of butter over medium heat. Add onions and mushrooms and sauté until the onions are slightly golden in color. Remove from the pan and set aside.

4 Add ground beef, hot sauce, Worcestershire sauce, and salt to the sauté pan. Cook until the meat is browned, making sure to let any liquid that releases from the meat evaporate. Add onions and mushrooms back to the pan. Stir to combine.

5 Remove any water that's accumulated in the baked bell peppers. Evenly stuff the ground beef mixture into each pepper.

6 If using cheese, top each pepper with it and pop them back in the oven long enough to melt the cheese.

CHILI DOG CHILI

SERVES 6

If you were to walk up to a hot dog stand and say, "I'd like a hot dog with no bun, extra chili, and a bunch of toppings," this is what you'd get. We like to spoon out a bit of adobo sauce from canned chipotle peppers in adobo sauce. It adds a smoky heat that you just can't duplicate with regular hot sauce. You can find chipotles in adobo sauce in the Latin or ethnic aisle of most grocery stores.

1 pound ground beef	TOPPING IDEAS
1 pound hot dogs, chopped	Sauerkraut
1 15-ounce can crushed tomatoes	Pickled jalapenos
1 4-ounce can diced green chilies	Yellow mustard
1 cup tomato sauce	Chopped onion
1 tablespoon adobo sauce	Pickle relish
1 teaspoon granulated garlic	Shredded cheese
1 teaspoon ground cumin	Diced avocado

1 In a large sauté pan, brown the ground beef and hot dogs.

2 Add the crushed tomatoes, green chilies, tomato sauce, adobo sauce, garlic, and cumin.

3 Let the chili simmer for 15 minutes to evaporate a bit of the liquid.

4 Top with a generous pile of your favorite hot dog toppings.

ALL-AMERICAN BURGER

SERVES 4

The all-American, classic, diner-style burger, complete with special sauce and a french fry bun.

FOR THE BUN

3 medium potatoes (3-inch diameter) cut into ¼-inch thick potato rounds

2 tablespoons duck fat, plus more for pan

1 tablespoon sesame seeds (optional)

Salt to taste

FOR THE BURGER

1 pound ground beef

½ yellow onion, diced

Salt and pepper to taste

FOR THE SPECIAL SAUCE

½ cup mayonnaise (page 262)

1 teaspoon tomato paste

2 teaspoons Worcestershire sauce

2 teaspoons prepared horseradish

¼ cup dill pickle chips, finely diced

Salt and pepper to taste

1 Preheat oven to 400°F.

2 Bring a large pot of water to a boil. Add potato rounds and cook for 5 minutes. They should still be firm, but not entirely cooked through.

3 Drain potatoes and pat dry.

4 On a baking sheet, toss potato rounds with duck fat and season with salt. Bake for 25 minutes, flipping once halfway through cooking. If desired, sprinkle with the sesame seeds after flipping.

5 While potatoes are baking, divide the ground beef into 8 equal balls and form the balls into patties. Season the patties with salt and pepper. Press diced onion onto the outside of each of the patties.

6 Heat a cast-iron skillet on medium-high and cook the burgers until they're done to your liking, about 2 to 3 minutes per side.

7 Mix all ingredients for the special sauce in a mixing bowl.

8 Serve burgers stacked between the potato buns, drizzled with special sauce, and layered with lettuce, onion, and tomato.

STEAK & EGGS TARTARE

SERVES 4

We used the mack daddy of all cow parts in this recipe: le filet mignon. But any cut of meat that takes to the grill will do just as well in this recipe.

FOR THE STEAK & EGGS

Butter for the pan

1½ pounds filet mignon
or other grilling steak (like sirloin)

4 eggs

Salt to taste

FOR THE TARTARE SAUCE

⅓ cup mayonnaise (page 262)

1 tablespoon Worcestershire sauce

1 teaspoon hot sauce

1 medium shallot, minced

1 tablespoon capers, chopped

1 tablespoon fresh parsley, minced

Salt to taste

1 Preheat oven to 400°F. Get out a baking sheet.

2 In a skillet or grill pan, melt a tablespoon of butter over medium-high heat. Season steaks liberally with salt and pepper. Sear until a brown crust has formed on both sides, about 4 minutes per side.

3 Place seared steaks on the baking sheet and place in the oven. Roast until the internal temperature of the steak is around 130°F for medium rare, about 10 to 15 minutes depending on the thickness of your meat.

4 Melt another tablespoon of butter in the pan and fry the eggs any which way you like 'em.

5 Make the sauce by whisking together all the Tartare Sauce ingredients.

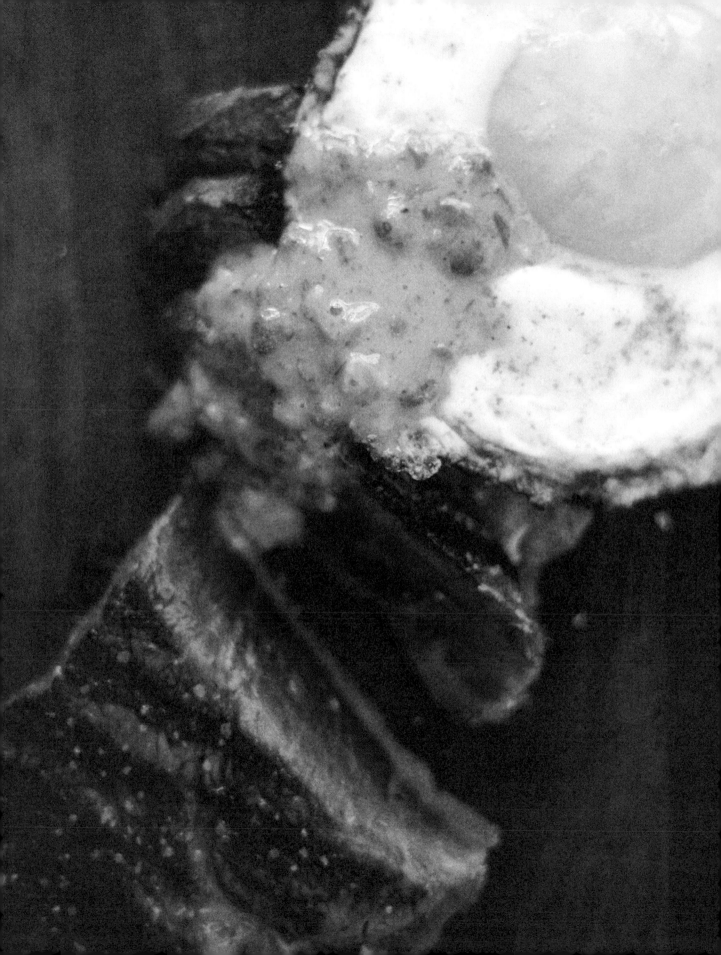

SLOPPY JOE MEATBALLS

SERVES 6

Does turning sloppy joe sandwiches into sloppy joe meatballs make eating this less sloppy? Reminds us of the equally existential thought: If a tree fell in the woods and no one was there to listen, would it still make a sound?

FOR THE MEATBALLS

Butter for the pan

1 large yellow onion, diced

2 pounds ground beef

3 tablespoons Worcestershire sauce

2 tablespoons wheat-free, reduced sodium soy sauce or coconut aminos

2 tablespoons apple cider vinegar

Salt and pepper to taste

FOR THE SAUCE

1 28-ounce can tomato sauce

½ cup water

2 tablespoons tomato paste

2 tablespoons Worcestershire sauce

1 tablespoon wheat-free, reduced sodium soy sauce or coconut aminos

1 tablespoon apple cider vinegar

½ cup roasted red peppers, diced

⅓ cup coconut sugar

Salt to taste

1 Preheat oven to 350°F.

2 In a medium pot, heat a tablespoon of butter over medium heat. Add the onion and sauté until cooked through.

3 Meanwhile, in a large bowl, combine the rest of the meatball ingredients. Once the onions are cooked, add half of them to the meatball mixture (keeping the other half in the pot). Use your hands or a scoop to form the meat into balls. Place the balls onto a baking sheet and bake until cooked through—depending on the size of your meatballs, about 15 to 20 minutes.

4 Meanwhile, add the sauce ingredients to the onions in the pot. Simmer the sauce while the meatballs bake in the oven.

5 Place the meatballs in the sauce and let them get cozy and hang out for a few minutes before serving.

CHICAGO DOG SKEWERS

SERVES 4

Pickled sport peppers can be hard to find. If you like heat, you can substitute pickled Tabasco peppers, which you'll find in pepper vinegar bottles, or even pepperoncinis.

FOR THE SKEWERS

- 1 pound hot dogs, cut into 2-inch pieces
- 1 pint cherry tomatoes
- ½ yellow onion, diced
- 8 dill pickle spears, cut into 2-inch pieces
- 30 sport peppers
- 1 tablespoon celery salt

FOR THE MARINADE

- ½ yellow onion, grated on a box grater
- ¼ cup yellow mustard
- 3 tablespoons apple cider vinegar

Celery salt to taste

1 Whisk marinade ingredients together in a small bowl and set aside. Next, combine hot dogs, tomatoes, diced onions, pickles, and peppers in a large bowl and add marinade. Toss to combine.

2 Thread hot dogs, tomatoes, diced onions, pickles, and peppers onto kebab skewers, alternating ingredients. If you're using bamboo skewers, it's a good idea to soak them in water for 20 minutes or so prior to skewering.

3 Grill over high heat just long enough to get some color, about 2 to 3 minutes. Flip and grill for another 2 to 3 minutes on the other side. Don't let the skewers sit on the grill too long or your tomatoes will fall apart.

4 Sprinkle kebabs with celery salt and serve.

SWEDISH MEATLOAF

SERVES 6

If you've ever been to that trendy, Scandinavian-based, famously budget-friendly furniture store, you've probably tried, or at least heard of, their Swedish meatballs. We've turned their deliciously famous meatballs into a Swedish meatloaf. Of course, if you're pressed for time, feel free to turn them back into meatballs and you'll have dinner on the table in way less than an hour.

FOR THE MEATLOAF

1   pound ground pork

1   pound ground beef

½   yellow onion, grated

1   teaspoon cardamom powder

1   teaspoon fresh nutmeg, grated

Salt and pepper to taste

FOR THE SWEET & SOUR CHERRY JAM

1   12-ounce bag frozen cherries

½   cup balsamic vinegar

½   cup beef stock

½   teaspoon fresh nutmeg, grated

1 Preheat oven to 350°F.

2 Place all the meatloaf ingredients in a large bowl, and using your handy-dandy hands, mix to combine thoroughly.

3 Shape the mixture into a loaf, and plop it into a standard loaf pan.

4 Bake until cooked through, about 45 minutes to an hour.

5 Meanwhile, combine the jam ingredients into a small sauce pot. Bring to a simmer and let cook until the liquids have reduced by about a third. Use a fork or potato masher to smash up the cherries.

6 Serve the meatloaf topped with the cherry jam.

BARBACOA POT ROAST
SERVES 6

A spicy Latin spin on the standard Sunday night pot roast.

5 pounds beef bottom round (chuck or shoulder will work, too)

1 chipotle pepper in adobo sauce (one pepper, not one can)

¼ cup apple cider vinegar

1 tablespoon ground cumin

2 teaspoons dried oregano

½ teaspoon ground allspice

2 teaspoons granulated garlic

2 cups beef stock

3 bay leaves, torn in half

3 carrots, peeled and chopped

2 yellow onions, peeled and chopped

Salt and pepper to taste

1 Preheat oven to 300°F. Generously season the beef with salt and pepper.

2 In a large dutch oven set over medium-high heat, brown the bottom round on all sides.

3 Meanwhile, make a spice paste by combining the chipotle pepper, vinegar, cumin, oregano, allspice, and garlic in a food processor. Buzz until smooth.

4 Once the beef has browned, turn the heat off. Add the spice paste, along with beef stock, bay leaves, carrots, and onions.

5 Wrap a sheet of aluminum foil over the dutch oven, prick a small hole or two in the top and stick the heavy beast in the oven. Let it cook until the meat is falling apart tender, about 5 to 6 hours.

6 Roughly shred the beef with a fork. Remove the bay leaves before serving.

SIDES & SALADS

ANTIPASTO SALAD

SERVES 2 TO 3

Giardiniera is a mix of pickled vegetables, most often containing cauliflower, carrots, and sweet peppers. You'll find it in the pickle aisle at most grocery stores. If not, you can substitute pickled sweet peppers (the southern classic, chow chow) or use a few handfuls of your favorite olives.

- 2 heads romaine lettuce, chopped
- 4 ounces shaved prosciutto
- 4 ounces salami
- 4 hard-boiled eggs, peeled and quartered
- 1 cup marinated artichokes
- 1 cup giardiniera

Don't worry about the exact measurements of the ingredients in the salad, just use the list as a guideline. Pile them on the lettuce in any configuration you'd like.

SWEET ROASTED RED PEPPER BASIL VINAIGRETTE

MAKES ABOUT 2 CUPS

- 1 whole roasted red pepper (from a jar)
- 2 tablespoons liquid from giardiniera or red wine vinegar
- 2 tablespoons extra virgin olive oil
- 1 tablespoon Dijon mustard
- 1 tablespoon honey
- 5 fresh basil leaves

Salt and pepper to taste

1 Buzz up all the ingredients in a blender.

2 Store in the fridge for up to 1 week.

BROCCOLI SALAD

SERVES 4

1 pound broccoli, chopped

8 ounces bacon, finely chopped

⅓ cup raisins

⅓ cup slivered almonds

3 tablespoons red wine vinegar

Salt and pepper to taste

1 With a sharp knife, cut off broccoli crowns from the stem. Then cut the crowns into smaller bite-sized pieces, and place in a large bowl.

2 Carefully cut away any leaves or stems from the remaining stalk of the broccoli, then cut the stalk into bite-sized pieces and add to the bowl of broccoli crowns.

3 Cook the bacon until crisp over medium heat in a medium sauté pan, stirring occasionally.

4 Add the crisped bacon and about half of the bacon drippings from the sauté pan to the bowl of broccoli. Add raisins, almonds, vinegar, plus salt and pepper to the bowl. Stir to combine.

5 Serve immediately, or refrigerate and serve cold.

CAESAR EGG SALAD
SERVES 4

⅓ cup mayonnaise (page 262)

1 tablespoon lemon juice

1 tablespoon Worcestershire sauce

1 tablespoon Dijon mustard

12 hard-boiled eggs

Salt and pepper to taste

1 To make clean-up easier, make the mayonnaise in a large serving bowl.

2 Whisk in lemon juice, Worcestershire sauce, and Dijon mustard. Season with salt and pepper.

3 Peel and chop up the hard-boiled eggs, and combine them with the Caesar dressing in the serving bowl. Serve cold.

TABOULI SALAD

SERVES 4

If Megan is at the table, this salad really only serves one.

1   pound tomatoes, cored, seeded, and finely chopped

1   English cucumber, chopped

½   red onion, finely diced

4   tablespoons lemon juice

4   tablespoons extra virgin olive oil

3   tablespoons fresh mint, chopped

Salt and pepper to taste

1 Combine ingredients in a large bowl.

2 Refrigerate, stirring occasionally until cold.

TEQUILA, LIME & GREEN ONION SLAW

SERVES 6

If you're hankering for something tangy, creamy, and crunchy, this slaw has your name written all over it.

½ cup mayonnaise (page 262)

4 green onions, thinly sliced

3 tablespoons lime juice

2 tablespoons tequila

1 2-pound green cabbage

Salt to taste

1 In a large bowl, whisk together mayonnaise, green onions, lime juice, tequila, and salt. Taste and adjust seasoning, remembering that this should be seasoned relatively assertively because when we add the cabbage, the flavor will dilute.

2 Remove any ugly or damaged outer leaves from the cabbage. Cut the cabbage in half lengthwise. Cut out the fibrous core. Place the cabbage, cut side down, and slice it into very thin strips.

3 Add the cabbage to the mayonnaise mixture. Toss to combine.

4 Refrigerate and let marinate at least 30 minutes before serving.

MOROCCAN CARROT SALAD

SERVES 4

Put this salad together faster by buying store-bought shredded carrots.

1   pound carrots

3   tablespoons extra virgin olive oil

2   tablespoons fresh garlic, minced

1   tablespoon fresh mint, minced

2   tablespoons apple juice concentrate

2   tablespoons white vinegar

Salt to taste

1 Cut the tops and ends off of the carrots. Peel the carrots and discard the skins. Continue to peel the carrots until you've whittled them down as far as you can.

2 Place the carrots in a large bowl, and add olive oil, garlic, mint, apple juice concentrate, vinegar, and salt.

3 Refrigerate until cold, stirring occasionally to coat the carrot peels.

ROASTED SQUASH & BEET SALAD

SERVES 4

We use canned beets for this recipe, just for speed and the fact that we didn't want our hands to look like we just committed a felony. If you're up for the mess, go ahead and roast and peel your own beets.

1   large butternut squash

2   15-ounce cans whole beets

2   tablespoons extra virgin olive oil, plus more for roasting the squash

3   tablespoons orange juice

1   tablespoon fresh tarragon, minced

    Salt and pepper to taste

1 Preheat oven to 400°F. Line a baking sheet with a silicone pat or parchment paper.

2 Peel and cut the butternut squash, making sure you remove all the seeds from the bulbous part of the squash. Don't get too hung up on the stringy bits; those won't be noticeable once they're cooked. Cut the squash into small cubes, about 1-inch squares.

3 Place the squash on a baking sheet, and drizzle with olive oil and salt. Toss to coat. Roast until soft, about 15 to 20 minutes.

4 In serving bowl, whisk together olive oil, orange juice, tarragon, and some salt and pepper.

5 Cut the beets into quarters and place into serving dish.

6 Once the squash is soft, place in a serving bowl. Toss everything to combine.

MEDITERRANEAN PASTA SALAD

SERVES 4

4   large zucchinis

⅓   cup sun-dried tomatoes (preferably not packed in oil)

½   cup fresh basil leaves

1   tablespoon apple cider vinegar

4   tablespoons extra virgin olive oil

1   tablespoon fresh thyme

Salt and pepper to taste

1 Cut the ends off the zucchinis. Using a mandoline, slice each zucchini into long, thin planks. With a knife, cut the planks into very thin strips the size of spaghetti. Alternatively, you can buy a julienne vegetable peeler and go to town.

2 Combine sun-dried tomatoes, basil, vinegar, olive oil, thyme, and salt and pepper in a food processor. Buzz until smooth.

3 Pour the sun-dried tomato sauce over the zucchini "zoodles." Toss to combine. Keeps in the refrigerator for up to 4 days.

CHIMICHURRI SMASHED PLANTAINS

SERVES 4

These make mashed potatoes look like a big bowl of pale and wimpy.

FOR THE PLANTAINS

- 3 green plantains
- 3 garlic cloves, peeled
- 1 cup chicken stock

Salt to taste

FOR THE CHIMICHURRI

- 1 green onion
- 1 handful of fresh cilantro
- 1 tablespoon lime juice
- 1 teaspoon honey
- 2 tablespoons extra virgin olive oil

Salt to taste

1 Bring a large sauce pot of water to a boil.

2 Meanwhile, cut the ends off of the plantains. From top to bottom and around all the sides, score the skin of the plantains. Get your fingers underneath the score marks of the skin and gently pull the skin up and away from the flesh of the plantain.

3 Roughly chop the peeled plantains. Place the plantains and garlic cloves in the boiling water and cook until soft, about 10 minutes.

4 As the plantains boil, make the chimichurri by buzzing the ingredients in a food processor.

5 Drain the water from the plantains (doesn't need to be perfect), and add the chicken stock. Using a potato masher, mash the plantains until smooth. Swirl in the chimichurri sauce.

6 Serve immediately. These have a tendency to stiffen up as they cool, so if you need to re-heat them, place them in a sauce pot, along with a few splashes of chicken stock. Stir everything around and the plantains will loosen back up.

MAPLE, ORANGE, CHIPOTLE SWEET POTATO CRISP

SERVES 6 TO 8

FOR THE FILLING

2   pounds sweet potatoes

2   tablespoons butter

½   cup coconut milk

1   chipotle in adobo sauce

¼   cup maple syrup

1   tablespoon orange zest

3   tablespoons orange juice

Salt to taste

FOR THE TOPPING

2   tablespoons butter

¼   cup maple syrup

¼   cup coconut sugar

1   tablespoon orange juice

1   teaspoon vanilla extract

¼   teaspoon salt

2   cups pecans

1 Preheat oven to 350°F.

2 Bring a large soup pot filled with water to a boil. Meanwhile, peel and chop the sweet potatoes. Place into the boiling water and cook until tender, about 10 minutes.

3 To make the topping, melt butter in a large skillet, and add maple syrup, coconut sugar, orange juice, vanilla extract, and salt. Heat until the mixture starts to bubble, and let cook for about 2 minutes. Add pecans and stir to combine.

4 Beat the boiled sweet potatoes with an electric mixer fitted with a paddle attachment. Add in the rest of the filling ingredients and mix until smooth.

5 Pour the sweet potato filling into a 2-quart casserole dish, then add the pecan mixture. Bake until the sides of the casserole dish are bubbly, about 30 minutes.

COCONUT CURRY CHOWDER

SERVES 4

Make sure to look for sweet or mild curry powder. If not labeled as such, read the ingredient list and see if there are any chili powders involved. Hot curry powder does exist, and if substituted one-for-one in this recipe, could lead to a mouth-scorching surprise.

Coconut oil for the pan

2 teaspoons cumin seeds

2 teaspoons brown mustard seeds

1 tablespoon fresh, minced ginger

1 yellow onion, diced

4 garlic cloves, minced

1 tablespoon sweet yellow curry powder

1 tablespoon garam masala

2 14-ounce cans full-fat coconut milk

½ cup chicken stock

2 tablespoons lime juice

Salt to taste

1 In a medium-sized soup pot, melt the coconut oil over medium heat. Add the cumin and mustard seeds. Let them dance around the pot for a minute or two and then add the ginger, garlic, and onion. Sauté until onion is cooked through.

2 Add the curry powder and garam masala powder. Dump in the coconut milk, chicken stock, and lime juice. Whisk everything to combine.

3 Once the chowder has come to a simmer, it's ready to serve. Garnish with a sprinkle of sweet curry powder.

MUSTARD ROASTED ASPARAGUS

SERVES 4

Why they call whole grain mustard what they do has always made me scratch my head. Say you want to make your own mustard (yeah, yeah, we're just saying), you would look for and buy mustard seeds, not mustard "grains." So just to be clear, whole grain mustard is not made from grains.

2   pounds asparagus

Extra virgin olive oil

1   tablespoon Dijon mustard

1   tablespoon whole grain mustard

1   tablespoon prepared horseradish

Salt to taste

1 Preheat oven to 375°F.

2 Chop off the rough, woody bottom of the asparagus stalks and discard. Lay out asparagus on a baking sheet and coat with olive oil.

3 In a bowl, whisk together the mustards and horseradish. Pour mixture over the asparagus and use your hands to thoroughly coat.

4 Roast asparagus about 15 to 18 minutes, until soft but not mushy. Toss halfway through cooking. Serve hot out of the oven.

BABA GHANOUSH GRATIN

SERVES 6 TO 8

This is an intensely flavorful side dish, also one that would be a great stand-alone main dish for Primal/paleo vegetarians.

Extra virgin olive oil

3 large eggplants

2 large red onions, diced

4 garlic cloves, peeled and chopped

¼ cup raisins

1 tablespoon tahini

1 tablespoon lemon juice

1 14-ounce can coconut milk

2 teaspoons tapioca flour

¼ teaspoon ground cinnamon

¼ teaspoon ground cumin

¼ teaspoon ground allspice

¼ teaspoon grated nutmeg

¼ teaspoon cayenne pepper

Salt to taste

Cilantro or mint leaves, chopped (optional)

1 Preheat oven to 350°F.

2 Peel the skin off the eggplants and cut into 1-inch-thick slices. Place the slices on a baking sheet, drizzle with olive oil, and bake until they are slightly browned around the edges and look slightly dried out, about 15 to 20 minutes.

3 Meanwhile, in a sauté pan, heat a few tablespoons of olive oil over medium heat. Add in the onion and garlic. Cook until tender, about 10 minutes.

4 Combine the sautéed onion, garlic, tahini, lemon juice, raisins, coconut milk, tapioca flour, spices, and salt in blender. Purée until smooth, and salt to taste.

5 To assemble, layer the gratin in a 13 x 9 x 2-inch baking dish. Begin with the eggplant rounds on the bottom, then add a layer of the purée. Continue to layer until all the ingredients are used.

6 Place in the oven and bake until the gratin starts to bubble around the edges, about 20 minutes. Garnish with cilantro or mint leaves.

BROWNED BUTTERNUT SQUASH & SAGE PURÉE

SERVES 6

Don't shortcut the process of making the browned butter. It is truly worth the patience and time it takes. You cannot buy this flavor.

Extra virgin olive oil

2 medium butternut squashes

½ cup butter

1 tablespoon lemon juice

3 tablespoons fresh sage, chopped

½ cup chicken stock

Salt and pepper to taste

1 Preheat oven to 400°F.

2 Cut the stem and bottom off the squashes. Peel off the skin and chop the flesh into chunks. Scoop out and discard the seeds. Don't worry about the stringy bits; they'll get blended away in the blender. Place the butternut squash chunks on a baking sheet and drizzle with olive oil. Bake until soft. Depending on how small or big your chunks are, that could be anywhere from 15 to 45 minutes.

3 Meanwhile, make the browned butter. Melt the butter in a sauté pan over low heat. You'll hear it start to crackle and see it start to foam as it slowly turns brown in color—should take about 15 or 20 seconds. Add lemon juice and sage. Let the sage fry up a bit, about 30 seconds, before removing the pan from heat.

4 Once the squash is cool enough to handle, combine with the browned butter and chicken stock in blender. Buzz until smooth, and season with salt and pepper.

CURRIED CREAMED SPINACH

SERVES 2

Curry and coconut milk go together like spinach and cream. We took the best of both worlds and smacked them together to make a super fast and nutritious side dish. Try using a package of frozen chopped spinach (that's been thawed and well squeezed) for a more budget-friendly option.

- 1 tablespoon extra virgin olive oil
- 5 ounces baby spinach leaves
- 4 tablespoons full-fat coconut milk
- ½ teaspoon mild or sweet curry powder

Salt to taste

1 In a large sauté pan, heat olive oil over medium heat and add spinach. Stir spinach around until it begins to wilt. Continue to cook about 2 more minutes to evaporate excess liquid.

2 Add the coconut milk, curry powder, and salt. Stir to combine and cook for about 1 minute. Taste and add more curry if you'd like.

ROOT RISOTTO

SERVES 2

Though celery root won't win any beauty contests, it shines in many other facets. With a low-starch content matched with a long shelf life and a clean, celery flavor—sometimes it's what's on the inside that's most delicious...we mean, that counts most.

Butter for the pan

1 large celery root (also commonly called celeriac)

1-2 cups chicken stock

Salt to taste

1 Slice the top and end off your celery root. Peel with a sharp knife and cut into quarters.

2 Using the grater attachment on your food processor, grate the celery root.

3 In a large sauté pan, heat a few tablespoons of butter over medium heat. Add the grated celery root and cook, stirring frequently for about 5 minutes.

4 While stirring, add in the chicken stock, about $1/3$ cup. When the stock is mostly absorbed, add a little more. Continue to add stock $1/3$ cup at a time until the celery root risotto has reached a creamy texture and is soft to the bite, about 10 minutes. Season with salt.

5 You may or may not need all the stock that's called for in this recipe, so it's important to taste as you go, making sure the texture and creamy mouth feel of the celery root is just where you want it.

RANCH POTATO SALAD

SERVES 6

Looking for lower carb? Substitute hard-boiled eggs for a creamy Ranch Egg Salad.

2   pounds Yukon gold potatoes

Ranch Dressing (page 261)

1   tablespoon salt

1 Peel and chop the potatoes into 1-inch chunks. Place in a large soup pot, filled with enough water to cover the potatoes. Add salt. Crank the heat up to high, and bring to a boil. Continue to boil until the potatoes are tender enough to be pierced by a fork, about 15 minutes.

2 Meanwhile, make the Ranch Dressing and place in serving bowl.

3 Once the potatoes are tender, drain the water and place in the serving bowl. Toss to combine and stick in the fridge to chill. Serve cold.

SNACKS

ROSEMARY & GARLIC PARSNIP CHIPS
SERVES 2 TO 4

Toss the chips about every five minutes while cooking so they'll get evenly crispy and crunchy.

1 pound parsnips

2 tablespoons fresh rosemary, minced

2 tablespoons fresh garlic, minced

Extra virgin olive oil

Salt to taste

1 Preheat oven to 350°F.

2 With a potato peeler, peel the outer skins of the parsnips and discard. Continue peeling until you've whittled the parsnip down to nothing but a nub.

3 Lightly grease a baking sheet with olive oil. On the baking sheet, toss the parsnip shavings with the minced rosemary and garlic along with a few tablespoons of olive oil and a hefty pinch of salt.

4 Bake until crispy, tossing occasionally for about 25 minutes.

BLOODY MARY PICKLED TOMATOES

MAKES 2 QUARTS

With its roots in Sunday brunch and the post-debauchery remedy of choice, the Bloody Mary cocktail is a favorite of many. We've un-cocktailed the drink and thrown in some fresh cherry tomatoes. The result is an awesome anytime snack.

- 1 pound cherry or grape tomatoes
- ¼ cup white vinegar
- ¼ cup lemon juice
- 1 tablespoon salt
- 1 tablespoon coconut sugar

IN EACH QUART SIZED JAR, ADD:

- 1 tablespoon prepared horseradish
- 1 tablespoon hot sauce
- 1 tablespoon Worcestershire sauce
- 1 tablespoon celery seeds

1 Cut the tomatoes into quarters and place them in canning jars.

2 Combine vinegar, lemon juice, salt, and sugar in a sauce pan. Cook over medium-low heat until the sugar and salt dissolve.

3 Pour vinegar solution into the jars.

4 Add in horseradish, hot sauce, Worcestershire sauce, and celery seeds. Fill the jar the rest of the way with water.

5 Seal the jars, give them a good shake, and place in the fridge. Tomatoes will be ready to eat in one day. Keeps in fridge for up 5 days.

BENEDICT DEVILED EGGS

MAKES 24 HALVES

Take the best parts of eggs benedict and leave the rest behind. Buttery, smooth yolks topped with salty, crispy cured ham. If you can't find pancetta, you can substitute prosciutto or bacon.

12	eggs
4	tablespoons butter, melted
¼	teaspoon cayenne pepper
5	slices pancetta
	Salt to taste

1 Preheat oven to 350°F.

2 Place eggs in a large pot of water and bring water to a boil. Turn the heat down to low and continue to cook until the eggs are hard-boiled, about 11 to 12 minutes. Remove eggs from the water and place in an ice bath (a bowl full of water and ice). The ice bath will stop the cooking and make the eggs easier to peel.

3 Meanwhile, place the pancetta slices on a baking sheet and bake in the oven until crispy, about 10 minutes. Crumble the crispy pancetta and set aside.

4 Peel the eggs and slice them in half lengthwise. Scoop the yolks out into the bowl of an electric stand mixer fitted with whisk attachment. Add the melted butter, cayenne pepper, and salt. Whisk until smooth.

5 Fill the egg white cavities with the yolk mixture, and top with the crumbled, crispy pancetta.

6 Serve close to room temperature as the yolk filling will harden when completely chilled.

PIZZA BITES

The prebake step of the pepperoni is super important if you want a crispy pepperoni "crust." Once you top the pepperonis they just don't crisp up much...

    8   ounces pepperoni slices

    1   cup Pizza Sauce (page 263 or store-bought)

    Toppings of choice

1 Preheat oven to 400°F. Lay the pepperoni slices on a baking sheet lined with parchment paper and bake until crispy—about 4 minutes each side. Start prepping your toppings while the pepperonis are in the oven.

2 Place a spoonful of pizza sauce on each pepperoni slice and top with your toppings.

3 Place the baking sheet back in the oven, and let the toppings get warm and melty, anywhere from 5 to 10 minutes.

All the toppings should be sliced, chopped, or diced super, super small and thin. Since you're making little petite pizzas and they're only getting a few minutes of oven time, you want make sure they're small enough to get cooked through.

TOPPING IDEAS

olives • peppers • onions

bacon • mushrooms

sausage • pineapple • ham

pesto • proscuitto • dried figs

artichokes

LUNCH•ABLE

One of the most frequently asked questions we get is, "What the heck can I eat for lunch?" We always answer that we eat dinner's leftovers. But obviously, that isn't going to cut it 100 percent of the time. Easily found grocery store items that you can whip together in a hurry without a lot of fuss or prep involved makes eating Primal/paleo more lunch-able.

FAJITA
roast beef • salsa • onion • bell pepper • avocado • cilantro

ITALIAN
ham • salami • mustard • lettuce • onion • banana peppers • olive oil • dried oregano

SOUTHWEST CLUB
chicken or turkey • bacon • avocado • hot sauce or salsa

BANH MI
ham • cucumber • carrot • avocado • green onion • cilantro • chili garlic sauce

PESTO CLUB
chicken or turkey • pesto (or basil leaves) • bacon • lettuce • onion

REUBEN
corned beef or pastrami • spicy mustard (or thousand island) • sauerkraut

HAMBURGER
roast beef • lettuce • tomato • onion • dill pickle • yellow mustard

FRENCHY
ham • mango chutney • sliced apple • red onion

HORSEY
roast beef • prepared horseradish • lettuce • red onion

BACON & GUACAMOLE PEPPER POPPERS

SERVES 4

Only a few ingredients needed for this super easy and extremely tasty recipe. Plus no oven required! Make them for yourself without feeling guilty—all the necessary food groups are provided in one convenient package.

1 pound baby bell peppers

3 Haas avocados

2 tablespoons lime juice

½ teaspoon chili garlic sauce or Sriracha

Salt to taste

½ pound sliced bacon, cut into strips

1 Heat a large skillet over medium heat. Add bacon and cook until browned, then remove from pan and let drain on a plate lined with paper towels.

2 Cut each pepper in half lengthwise and remove the white membrane and seeds. Place on a serving plate or baking sheet.

3 In a bowl, mash together avocados, lime juice, chili garlic sauce, and salt.

4 Use a spoon to stuff the guacamole into the halved peppers. Top with crispy bacon.

5 Serve immediately or store in the refrigerator. Wait to crisp up the bacon and top the peppers with it until you're ready to serve, otherwise the bacon will get mushy and lose its lovely crunch.

CHEESE CRACKERS

MAKES ABOUT 2 DOZEN CRACKERS

These are quite addictive, so be prepared to inhale. And if you aren't prone to sharing, you should eat these hunched over in the back of a closet, where no one can find you.

¼ cup tapioca flour

1 tablespoon coconut flour

4 ounces cheddar cheese, shredded

4 tablespoons butter, softened

¼ teaspoon onion powder

¼ teaspoon powdered mustard

1 teaspoon baking soda

1 Preheat oven to 350°F.

2 Combine all ingredients in a food processor. Buzz until a ball of dough has formed.

3 Line a baking sheet with a silicone pat or parchment paper. Shape dough into 1-inch balls. Place balls on the baking sheet, leaving about 3 inches of space between each.

4 Bake until the edges have slightly browned, about 10 minutes.

BEEF JERKY THREE WAYS

FOR THE BEEF

1   pound london broil

CHIPOTLE LIME JERKY

1   chipotle pepper in adobo

2   tablespoons adobo sauce

1   tablespoon lime zest

1   tablespoon lime juice

2   tablespoons honey

1   teaspoon salt

BREAKFAST JERKY

½   teaspoon dried sage

½   teaspoon dried thyme

½   teaspoon red pepper flakes

¼   teaspoon cayenne pepper

½   teaspoon ground black pepper

½   cup beef stock

JAMAICAN JERK JERKY

1   teaspoon molasses

2   teaspoons white vinegar

1   tablespoon lime zest

½   teaspoon onion powder

½   teaspoon cayenne pepper

½   teaspoon red pepper flakes

½   teaspoon dried thyme

½   teaspoon ground black pepper

½   teaspoon ground allspice

½   teaspoon ground coriander

½   teaspoon powdered ginger

1   teaspoon salt

1 Place beef in freezer for 30 minutes. The colder the meat, the easier it is to cut in thin slices. Once it's semi-solid, slice the beef against the grain into thin strips.

2 Prepare any of the flavors listed to the left by combining the ingredients together in a food processor and blending until smooth. Each spice mixture makes enough for 1 pound of beef.

3 In a zip-top plastic bag, toss the beef strips with the spice mixture, making sure to coat the meat entirely.

4 Place beef in dehydrator and dry to manufacturer's recommendations.

5 Store between pieces of waxed paper at room temperature for up to 2 days. Wrap in plastic and refrigerate to store for up to 1 week.

BARBECUE FAUXTATO CHIPS

SERVES 2 TO 3

FOR THE CHIPS

- 1 large jicama
- 2 cups palm shortening

FOR THE BARBECUE SPICE BLEND

- 1 tablespoon coconut sugar
- 1 teaspoon salt
- 1 tablespoon smoked paprika
- 1 teaspoon granulated garlic
- 1 teaspoon mustard powder
- ¼ teaspoon cayenne pepper

1 Cut off the top and bottom of the jicama. Cut the jicama in half lengthwise. Peel off the skin with a potato peeler. Use a mandoline to slice the jicama as thinly as possible.

2 In a large sauce pot, melt the palm shortening and get the temperature to hover around 250–275°F. (You will need an oil or candy thermometer to help keep the temperature constant.)

3 In small batches, place the jicama slices in the hot oil, flipping them every so often, and fry until slightly brown around the edges, about 5 minutes per batch. Remove the chips and place onto a wire rack set on a baking sheet.

4 Combine the ingredients for the spice blend, and sprinkle over the fried chips.

OLIVE OIL FOCACCIA
MAKES 8 SLICES

FOR THE FOCACCIA

- ½ cup very warm water
- 1 teaspoon honey
- 1 ¼-ounce package Fleischmann's RapidRise yeast
- 1 tablespoon olive oil
- 1 egg
- ½ cup tapioca flour
- ½ cup potato starch
- 3 tablespoons coconut flour
- 1 teaspoon baking powder
- ½ teaspoon salt

FOR THE TOPPING

- 1 tablespoon extra virgin olive oil
- ¼ cup kalamata olives, chopped
- 1 sprig fresh rosemary, chopped

Salt to taste

1 Place water and honey in a medium bowl. Sprinkle in yeast. Whisk to combine. Let sit for a minute or two to allow yeast to activate (noticeable by the pale foam that will develop on the surface of the water). Whisk in the olive oil and egg.

2 In a large bowl, whisk tapioca flour, potato starch, coconut flour, baking powder, and salt together.

3 Pour the wet ingredients into the dry ingredients. Whisk thoroughly.

4 Preheat oven to 325°F. Place a sheet of plastic wrap tightly over the bowl of dough, and let rise for 30 minutes in a warm place such as the top of the pre-heating oven or in a warm, draft-free corner.

5 Line a baking sheet with a silicone pat or parchment paper. Place the dough on the prepared baking sheet and shape into a 1-inch-thick disc.

6 Use your fingers to create dimples on the top of the dough. Drizzle olive oil on top, and sprinkle with chopped olives, rosemary, and a hefty sprinkle of salt.

7 Bake until the bottom of focaccia has browned, about 30 to 35 minutes.

EVERYTHING CRACKERS

MAKES ABOUT 3 DOZEN CRACKERS

FOR THE CRACKERS

1   cup tapioca flour

¼   cup potato flour

¼   cup potato starch

⅓   cup water

¼   cup high oleic sunflower oil, plus more for the pan

1   egg

FOR THE EVERYTHING SPICE TOPPING

1   teaspoon sesame seeds

1   teaspoon salt

1   teaspoon poppy seeds

1   teaspoon granulated garlic

1   tablespoon dehydrated onion flakes

1 Preheat oven to 400°F. Lightly grease a baking sheet with sunflower oil.

2 In a large bowl, whisk together tapioca flour, potato flour, and potato starch.

3 In another bowl, whisk together water, oil, and egg.

4 Pour the wet ingredients into the dry and whisk well to combine.

5 Knead the dough a few times, then use a rolling pin to roll the dough out until it's about ¼-inch thick. Sprinkle on the spice topping and cut into desired shapes.

6 Lay the crackers onto your prepared baking sheet and bake until crispy, about 15 to 18 minutes.

B-BUTTER

MAKES ABOUT 12 OUNCES

Our (extremely limited and unscientific) research shows that almost every household has at least one spouse or partner that's PBO, Peanut Butter Obsessed. In our house, it's the mister who's smitten with the pea paste. This recipe is an ode to him and those who share his nutty obsession.

- 8   ounces raw macadamia nuts
- 2   tablespoons tahini (sesame paste)
- 2   tablespoons sunflower seed butter
- 1   tablespoon honey
- 1   teaspoon salt

1 Preheat oven to 300°F.

2 Place macadamia nuts on a baking sheet and toast until slightly brown, making sure to shake the pan several times during cooking, about 20 minutes.

3 Add toasted macadamia nuts, tahini, sunflower butter, honey, and salt to a food processor and buzz until smooth.

4 Store in the fridge for up to 1 month.

TRAIL MIX CUPS

MAKES ABOUT 24

Trail mix almost always consists of something sweet, something salty, something crunchy, and something chewy. Whenever Megan eats trail mix, she almost always scrounges around the bag, meticulously selecting and creating the perfect mouthful of flavors and textures. In this recipe, we combine those most glorious ingredients into a two-bite package, and all the hard work is done.

1½ cups chocolate chips

APRICOT & ALMOND

¼ cup almonds, roughly chopped

¼ cup dried apricots, finely chopped

CHERRY PISTACHIO

¼ cup pistachios, roughly chopped

¼ cup dried cherries, chopped

1 teaspoon lemon peel, grated

CASHEW COCONUT LIME

¼ cup cashews, roughly chopped

¼ cup unsweetened dried coconut

1 teaspoon lime zest

BANANA PECAN

¼ cup dehydrated bananas, chopped

¼ cup raw pecan pieces, chopped

1 Line a mini-muffin pan with paper liners.

2 To melt the chocolate, microwave the chocolate chips in a heat-safe bowl in 15 second intervals, stirring well between intervals. The chocolate should be melted in about 45 seconds.

3 Spoon about a tablespoon of melted chocolate into each muffin liner.

4 Each flavor combination makes enough for about six trail mix cups. So increase or omit as desired.

5 Toss together the nuts and fruit (and zest). Place mixture into the melted chocolate and use a spoon to make sure all of the goodies are glued down into the melted chocolate.

6 Place the muffin pan in the refrigerator until the chocolate is firm.

JUICY JIGGLERS

SERVES 6 TO 8

Yay for homemade gelatin snacks! This easy-to-make after-school snack works wonderfully with all sorts and combinations of juices. Here are some great flavors to try:

Concord Grape, Peach and Mango, and Blueberry and Pomegranate

You can also play around with replacing half the water with a non-sweetened, flavored sparkling water. Flavors like Peach and Pear, Raspberry Lime and Orange Vanilla work wonderfully.

- 12 ounces frozen juice concentrate, thawed
- 24 ounces water, divided in half
- 2 tablespoons powdered gelatin

1 In a medium sauce pot, combine thawed juice concentrate and 12 ounces of water over high heat. Heat until the juice starts to simmer.

2 Meanwhile, add the other 12 ounces of water to a 13 x 9 x 2 baking dish. Uniformly sprinkle the gelatin over the water. Let sit for about 2 minutes.

3 Pour the hot juice mixture into the baking dish and whisk to combine.

4 Pop in the refrigerator and chill until firm. It'll be ready to eat in about 3 to 5 hours.

SWEETS

OPEN-FACED APPLE PIE
SERVES 6

FOR THE FILLING

2 tablespoons butter

2 tablespoons apple juice concentrate

1 teaspoon ground cinnamon

1 tablespoon lemon juice

2 tart apples, peeled and thinly sliced

FOR THE CRUST

1 cup tapioca flour

¼ cup coconut flour

6 tablespoons cold butter, plus more for the pan

1 egg, beaten

2 tablespoons apple juice concentrate

1 Preheat oven to 350°F. In a large sauté pan, reduce butter, apple juice concentrate, cinnamon, and lemon juice into a syrup, about 5 minutes. Add apples and stir to combine.

2 In a large bowl, whisk together tapioca and coconut flours. Cut butter into small cubes and using your fingers, rub the butter into the flour mixture until it is sandy in texture. Stir in egg and apple juice concentrate.

3 Lightly grease a baking sheet. Turn the dough out onto the baking sheet and press it into a circular shape, about ¼-inch thick. Pour the apples and all of its yummy juiciness on top, making sure to keep a 1-inch border around the edge of the dough. Push the border up around the apples, creating a sort of moat to catch all the syrup.

4 Bake until the crust is browned, about 30 minutes.

BLUEBERRY PASTRY PIES

MAKES SIX 4-INCH DOUBLE CRUST PIES

While Megan was growing up, her mother scratch-made pretty much everything the family ate, yet Megan couldn't wait to devour anything store-bought and vacuum sealed—most especially those frosted toaster pastries. Here, we offer a healthier, scratch-made version. Blueberry is super delicious, but also try swapping out the frozen blueberries and jam for strawberry or cherry.

FOR THE FILLING

- 1   cup frozen blueberries
- ⅓   cup 100 percent fruit blueberry jam
- 1   tablespoon lemon juice

FOR THE CRUST

- 1   cup tapioca flour, plus more for rolling out
- ¼   cup coconut flour
- 6   tablespoons cold butter
- 1   egg, whisked
- 2   tablespoons apple juice concentrate

1 Preheat oven to 350°F. In a small sauce pan, combine frozen blueberries, jam, and lemon juice. Let simmer until bubbly, about 5 to 6 minutes.

2 In a large bowl, whisk together tapioca and coconut flours. Cut the butter into small cubes, and using your fingers, rub the butter into the flour mixture until it looks sandy in texture. Stir in egg and apple juice concentrate.

3 Shape the dough into a disc, and coat it lightly with tapioca flour. Place the dough between 2 sheets of plastic wrap. Use a rolling pin to flatten out the disc until ¼-inch thick. Use a biscuit cutter (or the rim of a drinking glass) to cut out as many circular shapes as you can, re-rolling the dough out as many times as needed.

4 Line a baking sheet with a silicone pat or parchment paper. Place a dough circle on the baking sheet and fill with 1 tablespoon of blueberry filling. Place another dough circle on top and seal the edges with a fork or your fingers.

5 Bake until the crust has browned, about 30 minutes.

MAPLE PECAN PIE SQUARES

MAKES 16

We prefer to use Grade B maple syrup in most baked goods because it's a richer, more intense maple flavor, plus it's cheaper to buy than Grade A. Pecan meal, also called pecan nut flour, is just ground up pecans. You can find it in the baking aisle of most conventional grocery stores. If you're on a tight budget, think about buying pecan nut pieces instead of whole pecans; it's a much cheaper way to go.

FOR THE FILLING

2 tablespoons butter, melted

¾ cup maple syrup

2 eggs

½ teaspoon salt

1 cup pecans

FOR THE CRUST

1½ cups pecan flour

2 eggs

½ teaspoon salt

2 tablespoons maple syrup

1 Preheat oven to 350°F.

2 In a large bowl, whisk together the crust ingredients. Turn the dough out into an 8 x 8 x 2-inch baking dish. Use your fingers to press the crust evenly around the pan. Bake for 15 minutes.

3 Remove the crust from the oven and let it cool.

4 In a large bowl, whisk together butter, maple syrup, eggs, and salt. Pour the batter into the cooled pecan crust. Pour in the pecans.

5 Bake until the filling has set, about 20 minutes.

6 Once removed from the oven, let cool in the refrigerator before slicing into 2-inch squares.

MANGO ORANGE CREAM POPS

MAKES 6

Blend and freeze. A kid-friendly, old-fashioned ice cream truck favorite made super, super easy.

1	pound frozen mango chunks, thawed
½	cup orange juice (from about 3 oranges)
2	tablespoons orange juice concentrate
2	tablespoons orange zest
¾	cup coconut milk

1 Combine all ingredients into a blender. Buzz until smooth.

2 Pour into ice pop molds and freeze until solid, at least 4 hours but ideally overnight.

3 Remove the ice pops from their molds and store in the freezer, individually wrapped in plastic.

STRAWBERRY LEMONADE PUDDING

It's like summer in a cup—without the face-melting heat. Either let the pudding set in a large bowl and go from there, or portion the pudding into individual serving containers before placing in the refrigerator to set.

1 teaspoon powdered gelatin

8 egg yolks

½ cup lemon juice

½ cup 100 percent fruit strawberry jam

½ cup butter, cut into chunks

¼ teaspoon salt

½ cup coconut milk

1 Fill a very small bowl with 2 tablespoons of lukewarm water. Sprinkle the gelatin as uniformly as possible over the water. This is called "blooming" the gelatin. The water and powdered gelatin will combine to form a paste.

2 In a medium sauce pot, whisk together the egg yolks, lemon juice, and strawberry jam over medium heat. Then whisk in the butter and salt.

3 Continue to whisk until the butter is melted and mixture is thick enough to coat the back of a spoon, about 6 minutes.

4 Turn the heat off. Whisk in the bloomed gelatin paste.

5 Pour mixture into a fine mesh strainer over a clean bowl, and stir in the coconut milk. Press a piece of plastic wrap onto the top of the pudding. Place in the fridge to firm up, about 3 hours.

6 Alternatively, place in the freezer for gelato.

CHERRY LIMEADE SORBETA

SERVES 4

A cross between a sorbet and a granita, this is tangy, sweet, and mouth-puckeringly delicious. If you're pressed for time, cut the purée with club soda or coconut water for a delicious liquid refresher.

    2   12-ounce bags frozen cherries, thawed

    2   tablespoons 100 percent fruit strawberry jam

    ¼   cup lime juice

1 Purée cherries, jam, and lime juice in blender.

2 Pour purée into a pie tin or freezer-safe dish.

3 Place dish in the freezer. Every 30 minutes or so, flake the purée with a fork until the shards are completely frozen through, about 2 hours.

4 Use an ice cream scoop to portion out the sorbeta.

5 It's best to serve this immediately, but if you have the sorbeta in the freezer for longer than 4 hours, make sure to set it out at room temperature for about 15 minutes before serving.

CHOCOLATE ALMOND GELATO

MAKES ABOUT 1 QUART

No ice cream maker needed here. This is the absolute creamiest low-sugar ice cream you will ever eat.

   6 egg yolks

   ¼ cup coconut sugar

   ¾ cup chocolate chips

   1 14-ounce can coconut milk

   ½ teaspoon almond extract

   1 teaspoon powdered gelatin

   Slivered almonds for garnish

1 It's important to make sure you have everything set up before you get started with this recipe. Have all of the ingredients close by or already measured out. Open the can of coconut milk, and place a fine mesh strainer over a clean bowl.

2 In a sauce pot, whisk together the egg yolks and coconut sugar over low heat. Continue whisking until the mixture thickens and you start to see tiny bubbles form, about 5 minutes.

3 Whisk in chocolate chips, coconut milk, and almond extract. Slowly sprinkle the gelatin over the mixture. Whisk to combine.

4 Continue to whisk until the mixture is warm to the touch.

5 Pour mixture through strainer to remove any cooked egg chunks. Transfer strained mixture into a freezer-safe container. Freeze for about 3 hours.

6 Let ice cream sit at room temperature for about 15 minutes before scooping. Garnish with almonds and serve.

CARAMELIZED BANANA MILKSHAKE

SERVES 4

Make sure you use spotty bananas for this recipe as they're naturally sweeter. Add a splash or two of dark rum for Bananas Foster in a glass.

- 4 bananas, peeled
- 2 tablespoons coconut sugar
- 1 14-ounce can coconut milk

1 Preheat oven on the broil setting, and place the oven rack about a quarter of the way down from the broiler. Line a baking sheet with a silicone pat or parchment paper.

2 Slice the bananas into coin shapes and lay them on the baking sheet. Sprinkle each coin with coconut sugar. Place the bananas in the oven, and broil until the sugar melts and caramelizes.

3 Remove the baking sheet from the oven, and let cool to room temperature. Place the baking sheet in the freezer until the bananas are frozen through, about 1 hour.

4 Add the frozen, caramelized banana coins and coconut milk into a blender and buzz until smooth.

THIN MINTS

MAKES ABOUT 30 COOKIES

Crispy, thin chocolate cookies, drenched in minty chocolate ganache. Store these babies in the freezer for the ultimate after-dinner mint.

FOR THE COOKIES

1	cup almond butter
2	eggs
¾	cup coconut sugar
1	teaspoon baking soda
½	cup cocoa powder
1	teaspoon vanilla extract

FOR THE MINT CHOCOLATE GANACHE

1½	cups chocolate chips
1	tablespoon coconut milk or cream
1	teaspoon peppermint extract

1 Preheat oven to 350°F.

2 Beat together the cookie ingredients using an electric mixer fitted with a paddle attachment.

3 Place the dough on a large piece of plastic wrap. Place another piece of plastic wrap, the same size as the first, on top. Use a rolling pin to roll the dough out between the plastic wrap as thinly as you can. Place the rolled out dough on a baking sheet, and pop in the fridge for 10 minutes to chill.

4 Once chilled, use a cookie cutter (or the rim of a drinking glass), to cut out circular shapes. Line a baking sheet with a silicone pat or parchment paper, then place the cut-out dough on the baking sheet, about 2 inches apart. Bake until set, about 10 minutes.

5 For the mint chocolate ganache, fill a medium sauce pot halfway with water. Place a metal or glass bowl over the top so it fits like a double boiler. Pour chocolate, coconut milk, and peppermint extract in the bowl. Turn the heat to medium-high. Whisk occasionally, until the chocolate melts and everything is mixed well. Reduce the heat to low. Taste and adjust for peppermint-iness.

6 Line two clean baking sheets with parchment paper or a silicone pat.

7 Plop the cookies one at a time into the ganache, flipping them over to coat completely. Schluff off any excess ganache. Grab the cookies by their sides (We don't want fingerprint evidence), and lay them on baking sheets. Place the baking sheets in the fridge or freezer to harden the ganache.

8 Once hardened, place cookies in an airtight container and store in the fridge or freezer.

CHOCOLATE COCONUT SCOUT COOKIES

MAKES 12

You know exactly what badge-earning, yearly cookie peddlers we're riffing off.

1¼ cup unsweetened coconut, shredded

⅓ cup coconut sugar

¼ cup coconut oil, melted

1 egg

1 teaspoon vanilla extract

¼ cup chocolate chips

1 Preheat oven to 350°F. Line a baking sheet with a silicone pat or parchment paper.

2 In a large bowl, whisk together coconut, coconut sugar, coconut oil, egg, and vanilla extract. Fold in chocolate chips.

3 Place a ring mold or biscuit cutter on your prepared baking sheet. Drop a heaping tablespoon-size ball of dough into a biscuit cutter or ring mold, and use your fingers to mash the dough into a uniform circular shape. Use the biscuit cutter as a guide. Repeat until all the dough is used up. Place cookies about 2 inches apart.

4 Bake until edges are golden brown, about 15 minutes. Let cookies cool before handling.

THICK & CHEWY CHOCOLATE CHIP COOKIES

MAKES 1½ DOZEN

- ½ cup butter, softened
- ¾ cup coconut sugar
- 1 egg
- ¼ teaspoon salt
- 1 cup tapioca flour
- ¼ cup coconut flour
- 1 teaspoon baking powder
- ½ cup chocolate chips

1 Preheat oven to 375°F. Line a baking sheet with a silicone pat or parchment paper.

2 In a small bowl, whisk together salt, tapioca flour, coconut flour, and baking powder. Set aside.

3 Beat together butter and sugar with an electric mixer fitted with the paddle attachment. Continue to beat until fluffy, about 2 minutes. Add the egg and beat to combine, scraping down the sides of the bowl as needed.

4 With the mixer on low, slowly add the dry ingredients. After mixing, fold in the chocolate chips.

5 Drop dough by rounded tablespoons at least 2 inches apart on baking sheet.

6 Bake for 12 to 15 minutes. Cool on sheet before removing.

THIN & CRISPY CHOCOLATE CHIP COOKIES

MAKES 1½ DOZEN

1 Preheat oven to 325°F. Line a baking sheet with a silicone pat or parchment paper.

2 In a small bowl, whisk together the salt, tapioca flour, coconut flour, and baking soda. Set aside.

3 Beat together the butter and sugar with an electric mixer fitted with the paddle attachment. Continue to beat until fluffy, about 2 minutes.

4 Turn the mixer on low and slowly add the dry ingredients, and then the water. Beat until the mixture combines. Fold in the chocolate chips.

5 Drop dough by rounded tablespoons at least 3 inches apart on baking sheet. Press the cookies flat with your hands or a fork.

6 Bake for 12 to 15 minutes. Cool on sheet before removing.

- ½ cup butter, softened
- ¾ cup coconut sugar
- ¼ teaspoon salt
- 1 cup tapioca flour
- ¼ cup coconut flour
- ¼ teaspoon baking soda
- 3 tablespoons water
- ½ cup chocolate chips

DOUBLE CHOCOLATE ESPRESSO COOKIES

MAKES 1½ DOZEN

½ cup butter, softened

¾ cup coconut sugar

1 egg

1 egg yolk

¼ teaspoon salt

2 tablespoons finely ground coffee

¾ cup tapioca flour

¼ cup coconut flour

¼ cup cocoa powder

1 teaspoon baking soda

½ cup chocolate chips

1 Preheat oven to 375°F. Line a baking sheet with a silicone pat or parchment paper.

2 Whisk together salt, coffee grounds, tapioca flour, coconut flour, cocoa powder, and baking soda in a large bowl. Set aside.

3 Beat butter and sugar with an electric mixer fitted with the paddle attachment for about 2 minutes, until fluffy. Then beat in the egg and egg yolk, scraping down the sides of the bowl as needed.

4 Turn the mixer down to low and slowly add the dry ingredients until combined. Fold in the chocolate chips.

5 Drop by rounded tablespoon at least 2 inches apart on baking sheet.

6 Bake for 12 to 15 minutes. Cool on sheet before removing.

CARROT CAKE CREAM PIES

MAKES 12 COOKIES OR 6 CREAM PIES

These treats are hard to beat. If you're in a hurry, you can completely forget about the cream pie filling, and you'll find yourself with delicious soft-baked carrot cake cookies. Or go all-out and make some of the most delicious bake-sale-worthy cream pies you've ever had.

FOR THE CARROT CAKE COOKIES

- 1   cup almond butter
- 2   eggs
- 1   cup grated carrots
- ⅓   cup maple syrup
- ¼   cup raisins
- ½   teaspoon baking soda
- ¼   teaspoon salt
- ¼   teaspoon ground cinnamon
- ¼   teaspoon grated nutmeg
- ¼   teaspoon ground cloves

FOR THE FILLING

- 1   cup palm shortening
- ⅓   cup honey
- 1   tablespoon orange zest
- 1   teaspoon vanilla extract

1 Preheat oven to 350°F.

2 Beat together cookie ingredients with an electric mixer fitted with a paddle attachment. Dough will be wet.

3 Drop heaping tablespoons of dough about 2 inches apart on cookie sheet lined with parchment paper or a silicone pat.

4 Bake about 14 to 16 minutes, until cookies puff but are still soft. Let cool before removing from sheet.

5 For the filling, beat the palm shortening, honey, orange zest, and vanilla extract with an electric mixer fitted with a whisk attachment until fluffy.

6 To make the cream pies, use a spoon to slather the filling onto the bottom of one cookie, then top with another cookie. Repeat until all the cookies are used.

7 Store cream pies in an airtight container at room temperature for up to 1 week.

BROWNIES

MAKES 16 BROWNIES

A marriage between cakey brownies and fudgy brownies, so no one feels left out.

- 2 tablespoons tapioca flour
- 3 tablespoons coconut flour
- 1 tablespoon cocoa powder
- ¼ teaspoon baking soda
- 1 cup chocolate chips or a 6-ounce chocolate bar cut into chunks
- ½ cup butter, plus more to grease pan
- ⅓ cup coconut sugar
- ¼ teaspoon salt
- 1 teaspoon vanilla extract
- 2 eggs

1 Preheat oven to 350°F. Lightly grease an 8 x 8 x 2-inch baking dish.

2 Whisk together tapioca flour, coconut flour, cocoa powder, and baking soda in small bowl.

3 Melt butter, sugar, and chocolate together in either a bowl (via the microwave) or a sauce pot (via the stove). Stir in vanilla extract and salt. Whisk in the eggs.

4 Pour the dry ingredients into the wet ingredients. Whisk to combine.

5 Pour the batter into baking dish, and bake until brownies are puffed in the center and not too jiggly when (gently) shaken, about 20 to 25 minutes. Allow to cool in pan before cutting into 2 x 2-inch squares.

DIRTY BLONDIES

MAKES 16 BLONDIES

For the creamed coconut used in this recipe, we prefer the Let's Do Organic brand, which comes in an airtight package. Because it contains a mixture of coconut oil and coconut meat solids, it has a thicker, creamier texture than the coconut butters you typically find in a jar.

1 7-ounce package creamed coconut (Let's Do Organic brand)

½ cup coconut sugar

2 eggs

1½ teaspoons vanilla extract

¼ teaspoon salt

½ teaspoon baking soda

1 Preheat oven to 350°F. Lightly grease an 8 x 8 x 2-inch baking dish.

2 Place creamed coconut in a bowl, and microwave in 30-second increments until it can be whisked into a smooth paste.

3 Whisk in sugar, eggs, vanilla extract, salt, and baking soda.

4 Pour the batter into the baking dish, and bake until slightly puffed and springy, about 22 to 25 minutes. Allow to cool in pan before cutting into 2 x 2-inch squares.

5 Refrigerate blondies for a denser mouth feel.

CARAMEL COCONUT CUPCAKES

MAKES 12

There's some serious coconut flavor packed in these cupcakes. If you have any leftover caramel, you can use it as a dip for fresh fruit.

FOR THE COCONUT CUPCAKES

- ½ cup coconut flour
- ½ cup tapioca flour
- 1 teaspoon baking soda
- 4 eggs
- ½ cup coconut oil, melted
- ⅓ cup coconut sugar
- ½ cup unsweetened applesauce
- 1 teaspoon coconut extract
- Toasted coconut for garnish

FOR THE COCONUT CARAMEL

- ⅓ cup maple syrup
- ⅓ cup honey (or coconut sugar for a darker caramel)
- ½ cup butter, softened
- 2 tablespoons coconut milk
- ¼ teaspoon salt

1 Preheat oven to 350°F. Line a standard muffin tin with liners.

2 Whisk together coconut flour, tapioca flour, and baking soda in a large bowl.

3 In another large bowl, whisk together eggs and coconut oil, then whisk in sugar, applesauce, and coconut extract.

4 Add the dry ingredients into the wet ingredients and whisk to combine.

5 Pour the batter into the baking dish, and bake until cupcakes are cooked through, about 22 minutes.

6 For the caramel, heat maple syrup and honey in a sauté pan over medium heat. Whisk occasionally, until the syrup starts to bubble, about 2 minutes. Whisk in the butter until it completely dissolves, then whisk in coconut milk and salt.

7 Pour the caramel into a bowl and place in the refrigerator to chill.

8 Dip the top of the cooled cupcakes into the chilled caramel to frost.

NO-BAKE GRANOLA BARS

MAKES 8 BARS

2½	cups unsweetened shredded coconut
1	cup B-Butter (page 206)
½	cup coconut oil, melted
⅓	cup honey
⅓	cup chocolate chips

1 Preheat oven to 350°F. Lay the shredded coconut in an even layer on a baking sheet. Toast until about a third of the coconut shreds look toasty brown. Remove from oven and cool.

2 Beat together B-Butter, coconut oil, and honey with an electric mixer fitted with a paddle. Fold in chocolate chips and toasted coconut.

3 Pour batter into an 8 x 8 x 2-inch baking dish.

4 Smooth the top of the batter, and place the dish in the refrigerator until hardened, about 3 hours. Cut into 4 x 2-inch bars.

5 Store in the refrigerator.

ALMOND HAPPINESS FUDGE

MAKES 16 PIECES
No lawsuit warranted with this name. Get it?

2   cups chocolate chips

¼   cup coconut milk

½   cup coconut oil

½   cup unsweetened shredded coconut

1   teaspoon coconut extract

2   tablespoons honey

¼   cup chopped almonds

1 Place a soup pot half full of water over medium-high heat and bring to a simmer. Next, combine chocolate chips and coconut milk in a heat-safe glass bowl and place over the pot to create a double boiler effect. Whisk until chocolate is completely melted, then remove from heat and allow to cool.

2 Beat together the coconut oil, coconut, coconut extract, and honey with an electric mixer fitted with a paddle attachment.

3 Once the chocolate-coconut milk reaches room temperature, pour it into an 8 x 8 x 2-inch baking dish. Add coconut mixture and swirl it together using a bamboo skewer or knife. Don't worry if the coconut mixture melts a little bit; it will firm back up.

4 Top with chopped almonds and place in the fridge for about 2 hours. Once firm, cut into 2 x 2-inch squares.

DEVIL'S FOOD SNACK CAKE

MAKES 16 SNACK CAKES

Inspired by a friend whose admitted weakness is those plastic-wrapped individual snack cakes that haunt the middle aisles of the grocery store. You can also bake these into cupcakes.

FOR THE CAKE

- ¼ cup coconut flour
- ⅓ cup tapioca flour
- 1 teaspoon baking soda
- 3 tablespoons cocoa powder
- 4 eggs
- ½ cup butter, melted, plus more for the pan
- ½ cup coconut sugar
- ½ cup unsweetened applesauce
- ½ cup chocolate chips

FOR THE CHOCOLATE BUTTERCREAM FROSTING

- ⅓ cup maple syrup
- ⅓ cup coconut sugar
- 4 egg yolks
- 5 tablespoons butter, softened
- 3 tablespoons cocoa powder
- ¼ teaspoon salt

1 Preheat oven to 350°F. Lightly grease an 8 x 8 x 2-inch baking dish.

2 Whisk together coconut flour, tapioca flour, baking soda, and cocoa powder in large bowl.

3 In another large bowl, whisk together eggs and butter, then whisk in sugar and applesauce.

4 Add the dry ingredients into the wet ingredients, and whisk to combine. Fold in the chocolate chips.

5 Pour batter into the baking dish, and bake until cooked through, about 25 minutes.

6 For the frosting, combine maple syrup and coconut sugar in a sauce pan over medium heat. Cook until the sugar has dissolved and starts to foam. Next, whip egg yolks with an electric mixer fitted with the whisk attachment until the color begins to pale. Then, while the mixer is running, slowly pour the hot sugar syrup into the egg yolks. Continue to whisk until the mixture has cooled (the mixing bowl will feel cool to the touch). Whisk in the softened butter, 1 tablespoon at a time, then whisk in the cocoa powder. If the buttercream frosting is too thin, it's likely because it's still warm, so place it in the fridge to firm up and become spreadable.

7 Frost the cake once completely cooled.

MAPLE BANANA SPICE CAKE

This spice cake will make you go bananas. Make sure you use very ripe, heavily spotted bananas. You'll know they're ready for baking when you don't want to peel and eat 'em.

½ cup butter, melted, plus more for the pan

½ cup maple syrup

1 cup mashed banana (about 2 large)

4 eggs

½ cup coconut flour

½ cup tapioca flour

1 teaspoon baking soda

1 teaspoon cinnamon

½ teaspoon powdered ginger

½ teaspoon grated nutmeg

½ teaspoon grounded cloves

1 Preheat oven to 325°F. Lightly grease a 1.5 quart oven-safe loaf pan.

2 In a large bowl, whisk together butter and maple syrup, then whisk in mashed banana and eggs.

3 In another large bowl, whisk together coconut flour, tapioca flour, baking soda, and spices.

4 Whisk the dry ingredients into the wet ingredients, and mix until thoroughly incorporated. Pour the batter into the loaf pan.

5 Bake until the edges are golden brown and the center of the cake is cooked through, about 50 minutes to 1 hour. Let the cake cool before removing from the pan.

BASICS

BREAD

MAKES 1 LOAF

This bread is best straight out of the oven. Wrap what's left of your loaf tightly in plastic wrap. Make toast or croutons (page 258) with the day-old loaf.

DRY INGREDIENTS

- ¾ cup tapioca flour
- ¾ cup potato starch
- ¼ cup coconut flour
- 2 teaspoons baking powder
- 1 teaspoon salt

WET INGREDIENTS

- ¾ cup very warm water
- 1 tablespoon honey
- 2 ¼-ounce packages Fleischmann's RapidRise yeast
- 3 tablespoons butter, melted
- 2 eggs
- 2 teaspoons powdered gelatin

1 Combine water and honey in a medium bowl. Sprinkle in yeast. Whisk together and let sit for a minute or two until the yeast is activated (noticeable by the pale foam that will develop on the surface of the water). Whisk in butter, eggs, and powdered gelatin.

2 Whisk together dry ingredients in a large bowl.

3 Pour the wet ingredients into the dry ingredients. Whisk thoroughly, making sure there are no lumps.

4 Preheat oven to 375°F. Place a sheet of plastic wrap tightly over the bowl and let the dough rise on top of the preheating oven or in a warm, draft-free corner for 1 hour.

5 Lightly grease a 1.5 quart glass loaf pan, and place dough in it.

6 Bake until the bread is lightly browned on all sides, about 45 minutes to 1 hour.

CROUTONS
MAKES 4 CUPS

4   cups day-old bread (page 256), cubed

6   tablespoons butter or extra virgin olive oil

2   teaspoons minced garlic

1   tablespoon fresh herbs (thyme, rosemary, etc.)

Salt and pepper to taste

1 Preheat oven to 400°F. Line a baking sheet with a silicone pat or parchment paper.

2 Melt butter over medium heat and add garlic. Sauté for 1 minute.

3 Place bread cubes in a bowl, and toss in garlic butter (and herbs if using) until evenly distributed.

4 Lay on prepared baking sheet. Bake until crispy, about 30 minutes.

PIZZA CRUST

1   cup tapioca flour

¼   cup potato flour

⅓   cup water

1   teaspoon powdered gelatin

1   egg

¼   cup high oleic sunflower oil or extra virgin olive oil, plus more for pan

Salt to taste

1 Preheat oven to 400°F. Grease a baking sheet or pizza tray.

2 In a large bowl, whisk together tapioca flour and potato flour.

3 In another bowl, sprinkle the powdered gelatin over the water. Add egg and oil, and whisk to combine.

4 Whisk the wet ingredients into the dry and knead until combined.

5 Use your hands (or a rolling pin) to press the dough out onto baking sheet.

6 Prebake the dough until it's crispy and golden brown, about 16 to 20 minutes. Remove from the oven and loosen the crust from the pan with a spatula.

CAESAR DRESSING

⅓ cup mayonnaise
(page 262)

2 teaspoons
Worcestershire
sauce

1 teaspoon Dijon
mustard

Juice of 1 lemon

1 tablespoon lemon
zest

Salt and pepper
to taste

BACON HONEY MUSTARD

⅓ cup bacon fat (leftover
from cooking bacon)

2 tablespoons
mayonnaise

⅓ cup yellow mustard

2 tablespoons honey

GREEK DRESSING

½ cup extra virgin
olive oil

Juice of 1 lemon

2 teaspoons dried
oregano

2 tablespoons red
wine vinegar

1 teaspoon Dijon
mustard

½ teaspoon
granulated garlic

Salt and pepper
to taste

RANCH DRESSING

½ cup mayonnaise
(page 262)

1 teaspoon red wine
vinegar

2 tablespoons
vegetable stock

1 teaspoon dried
thyme

1 teaspoon fresh dill,
minced

1 teaspoon onion
powder

Salt and pepper
to taste

THOUSAND ISLAND

⅓ cup mayonnaise
(page 262)

1 tablespoon
ketchup

2 teaspoons
Worcestershire
sauce

2 teaspoons
horseradish

1 teaspoon hot
sauce

½ cup pickles, diced

Salt and pepper
to taste

ITALIAN DRESSING

½ cup extra virgin
olive oil

¼ cup red wine or
balsamic vinegar

2 teaspoons Italian
seasoning

1 teaspoon
granulated garlic

1 teaspoon onion
powder

½ teaspoon paprika

Salt and pepper
to taste

MAYONNAISE

MAKES ABOUT 1 CUP

- 3 egg yolks
- 1 teaspoon Djion mustard
- 1 tablespoon lemon juice
- ¾ cup high oleic sunflower oil

Salt to taste

Combine egg yolks, mustard, and lemon juice in a large bowl. Begin to whisk and slowly, slowly, slowly drip-drop in the sunflower oil. Continue to slowly add the oil until a thick, creamy consistency has developed. Salt to taste.

WHAT DO YOU DO IF YOUR MAYONNAISE LOOKS LIKE CURDLED MUSH?

Scrape out the curdled mayonnaise and set aside. Add a fresh egg yolk plus a teaspoon of mustard back into the bowl. Whisk that up and slowly add in the curdled mayonnaise. This will re-emulsify the ingredients and no one will ever know.

PIZZA SAUCE

MAKES ABOUT 2 CUPS

- 1   15-ounce can tomato sauce
- 1   6-ounce can tomato paste
- ½   teaspoon granulated garlic
- 1   tablespoon Italian seasoning
- 1   teaspoon red pepper flakes

Salt and pepper to taste

Place all ingredients into a sauce pan. Whisk to combine. Bring to a simmer and cook for 5 minutes.

COUNTRY BREAKFAST SAUSAGE

TO 1 POUND OF GROUND MEAT ADD:

- 1 teaspoon dry mustard
- 1 teaspoon dried sage
- 1 teaspoon ground black pepper
- 1 teaspoon red pepper flakes
- 1 teaspoon smoked paprika
- ¼ teaspoon cayenne pepper
- 2 teaspoons salt

ITALIAN SAUSAGE
TO 1 POUND OF GROUND MEAT ADD:

1 tablespoon fennel seeds

1 tablespoon granulated garlic

1 tablespoon dried oregano

2 teaspoons salt

½ teaspoon red pepper flakes

¼ teaspoon cayenne pepper

CHORIZO SAUSAGE

TO 1 POUND OF GROUND MEAT ADD:

- 1 tablespoon paprika
- 1 tablespoon granulated garlic
- 2 teaspoons chili powder
- 1 teaspoon onion powder
- ½ teaspoon cinnamon
- ½ teaspoon cayenne pepper
- 2 tablespoons apple cider vinegar
- 2 tablespoons hot sauce
- 2 teaspoons salt

SALSA
MAKES ABOUT 3 CUPS

1   14.5-ounce can diced tomatoes

2   tablespoons lime juice

½   red onion

½   cup fresh cilantro

2   teaspoons granulated garlic

2   teaspoons salt

½   teaspoon allspice

Pulse in a food processor until desired chunkiness is reached.

RESOURCES

WHERE TO BUY

COCONUT FLOUR
Tropical Traditions TropicalTraditions.com
Let's Do Organic EdwardAndSons.com

TAPIOCA FLOUR/STARCH
ENER-G Ener-g.com
NOW Foods NowFoods.com

POTATO STARCH
ENER-G Ener-g.com

POTATO FLOUR
Bob's Red Mill BobsRedMill.com

POWDERED GELATIN
Great Lakes Gelatin GreatLakesGelatin.com

EXPELLER-PRESSED COCONUT OIL
Tropical Traditions TropicalTraditions.com

PALM SHORTENING
Tropical Traditions TropicalTraditions.com
Spectrum SpectrumOrganics.com

CREAMED COCONUT
Let's Do Organic EdwardAndSons.com

ALMOND BUTTER
Justin's Justins.com
MaraNatha No-Stir MaraNathaFoods.com

COCONUT SUGAR
Madhava MadhavaSweeteners.com
Wholesome Sweetners
WholesomeSweeteners.com

MEATS, BUTTER, LARD & SUCH
US Wellness Meats GrasslandBeef.com
Caw Caw Creek CawCawCreek.com
D'Artagnan Dartagnan.com

SHIRATAKI NOODLES
Miracle Noodle MiracleNoodle.com

FREE KNOWLEDGE

HEALTH-BENT
Health-Bent.com

Best paleo-friendly recipes ever. Full disclosure, we are totally biased.

The following sources reference the more scientific literature and will better inform you about macro/micro nutrition of whole foods, the dangers of grains, metabolism of carbs and sugar and dietary fat, and discuss the conventional wisdom myths that surround it:

MARK'S DAILY APPLE
MarksDailyApple.com

Seriously, one of the most sensible blogs about Primal/paleo as a lifestyle.

CHRIS KRESSER
ChrisKresser.com

Well-informed and easy to comprehend integrative health and wellness articles.

TOM NAUGHTON
Fathead-Movie.com

Hates bad science and rips apart studies in a fun-to-read way.

MELISSA MCEWEN
HuntGatherLove.com

Well-crafted articles about evolutionary biology and food.

DR. KURT HARRIS
Archevore.com

Currently dormant, there's still a wealth of science-y knowledge lingering on the site.

RECIP•EASY MENUS

A handy, no-stress compilation of meals, salads, sides, and sweets organized based on time, budget, and taste constraints.

30-MINUTE (OR LESS) MEALS, SALADS, AND SIDES

With some semi-speedy knife work, you can have these recipes on the table in about 30 minutes.

Pumpkin Chili & Zesty Guacamole

Curry Turkey Burgers & Mango Slaw

Steak & Eggs Tartare

Italian Fajitas & Bruschetta Salsa

Thai Chili Chicken Meatballs

Antipasto Salad

Spanakopita Soup

Smoked Salmon Hash

Western Omelette To Go

Broccoli Salad

Tequila, Lime & Green Onion Slaw

Mustard Roasted Asparagus

Coconut Curry Chowder

Pizza Bites

Moroccan Carrot Salad

Hot & Sour Chicken Noodle Soup

Chicago Dog Skewers

Sloppy Joe Meatballs

Chili Dog Chili

Tikka Masala Chicken Wings

Loaded Fauxtato Soup

Moo Shu Cabbage Cups

Gyro Taco Salad

Caprese Baked Eggs

Crawfish Étouffée

Tabouli Salad

Chimichurri Smashed Plantains

Curried Creamed Spinach

Bacon & Guacamole Pepper Poppers

Root Risotto

Lunch•Able

30-MINUTE SWEETS

Hankering for a quick sweet fix? These recipes are here to save the day.

Brownies

Chunky Monkey Muffins

Chocolate Chip Cookies

Carrot Cake Cookies

Coconut Cupcakes (no caramel)

Chocolate Coconut Scout Cookies

Dirty Blondies

Gingerbread Muffins

Cherry Almond Muffins (no streusel)

Double Chocolate Espresso Cookies

Maple Banana Spice Cake

Devil's Food Snack Cake (no frosting)

Cherry Limeade Sorbeta (as drink)

FEEDING A CROWD

These recipes are super easy to make in mass quantities and freeze, thaw, and re-heat beautifully.

Guacamole Pepper Poppers

Barbacoa Pot Roast

Best-Ever Pulled Pork

Cheese Crackers

Mediterranean Pasta Salad

Benedict Deviled Eggs

Thai Chili Chicken Meatballs

Caprese Baked Eggs

Antipasto Salad

Pumpkin Chili & Zesty Guacamole

Curry Turkey Burgers (made into meatballs)

Swedish Meatloaf (made into meatballs)

Moo Shu Cabbage Cups

Moroccan Carrot Salad

Mango Slaw

Chili Dog Chili

Tikka Masala Chicken Wings

Western Omelette To Go

Dairy-Free Strawberry Yogurt

Caesar Egg Salad

Chunky Monkey Muffins

Gingerbread Muffins

Chocolate Chip Cookies

Brownies

Strawberry Lemonade Pudding

Trail Mix Cups

Everything Crackers

Ranch Potato Salad

Mustard Roasted Asparagus

Coconut Curry Chowder

Seafood Chowder with Cheddar Biscuit

Loaded Fauxtato Soup

Tequila, Lime & Green Onion Slaw

Tabouli Salad

Chicago Dog Skewers

Buffalo Chicken Salad

Spanakopita Soup

Sausage & Eggs To Go

Honey Nut Crunch

Sweet Potato Crisp

BUDGET-FRIENDLY MEALS

These recipes are based on cheaper proteins, which are often the most flavorful.

Pumpkin Chili & Zesty Guacamole

Barbacoa Pot Roast

Best-Ever Pulled Pork

Coconut Curry Chowder

Spanikopita Soup (use beef)

Benedict Deviled Eggs

Thai Chili Chicken Meatballs

Caprese Baked Eggs

Moo Shu Cabbage Cups

Tikka Masala Chicken Wings.

Caesar Egg Salad

Chicago Dog Skewers

Seafood Chowder with Cheddar Biscuit

Loaded Fauxtato Soup

Chili Dog Chili

Buffalo Chicken Salad

Curry Turkey Burgers

Swedish Meatloaf

Western Omelette To Go

Sausage & Eggs To Go

Gyro Taco Salad (use beef)

Sloppy Joe Meatballs

VEGETARIAN FRIENDLY & ADAPTABLE

For a change of pace, remove the meats and meat-based stocks from these recipes.

Guacamole Pepper Poppers

Baba Ghanoush Gratin

Chimichurri Smashed Plantains

Cheese Crackers

Barbecue Fauxtato Chips

Benedict Deviled Eggs

Caprese Baked Eggs

Antipasto Salad

Shrimp Pad Thai

Root Risotto

Moo Shu Cabbage Cups (add more shrooms)

Moroccan Carrot Salad

Mango Slaw

Curried Creamed Spinach

Caesar Egg Salad

Hot & Sour Chicken Noodle Soup

Mediterranean Pasta Salad

Mustard Roasted Asparagus

Coconut Curry Chowder

Rosemary Parsnip Chips

Ranch Potato Salad

Cowboy Hashbrown Skillet

Loaded Fauxtato Soup

Bloody Mary Tomatoes

B-Butter

Butternut Squash Lasagna

Tequila, Lime & Green Onion Slaw

Tabouli Salad

Roasted Squash & Beet Salad

Brown Butternut Squash & Sage Purée

Pizza (sub ½ cup grated cheese for gelatin)

METRIC CONVERSIONS

For our friends outside the United States, we offer the following metric conversion charts. These are not exact equivalents, but have been rounded up or down for easier measuring and work well with most recipes in this cookbook. However, when preparing baked goods, we strongly recommend that you visit one of the many food-related websites or smartphone apps for a more precise conversion system specific to your country to ensure the best results. Regardless of the measuring system you use, the same system should be followed throughout.

U.S. MEASURES TO METRIC

(Based on the approach to metric measures developed in the United States and Canada)

Ounces to grams: multiply ounces by 28.35
Pounds to grams: multiply pounds by 453.5
Cups to liters: multiply cups (or fraction thereof) by 0.24
Fahrenheit to Celsius: subtract 32 from Fahrenheit temperature, multiply by 5, then divide by 9

Liquid Measures (Volume) May be used to calculate spices in small quantities	
1/8 teaspoon	0.5ml
1/4 teaspoon	1 ml
1/2 teaspoon	2 ml
3/4 teaspoon	4 ml
1 teaspoon	5 ml
1 tablespoon	15 ml
1/4 cup	60 ml
1/3 cup	75 ml
1/2 cup	125 ml
2/3 cup	150 ml
3/4 cup	175 ml
1 cup	250 ml
2 cups	500 ml
1 quart	1000 ml or 1 L
1 gallon	4 L

Weight Measures for solids, including meat, cheese, butter, flour, sugar	
1/2 ounce	15 g
1 ounce	25 g or 30 g
3 ounces	90 g
4 ounces	115 g or 125 g
8 ounces	225 g or 250 g
12 ounces	350 g or 375 g
16 ounces (1 pound)	450 g or 500 g
2-1/4 pounds	1 kg
5 pounds	2.5 kg

Oven Temperatures	
Fahrenheit	Celsius
300°	150°
325°	160°
350°	180°
375°	190°
400°	200°

NUTRITION INDEX

Recipe nutrition information is calculated per serving. Carbohydrate counts include sugars and starch. All nutrition information is estimated based on online nutrition data.

	CALORIES	FAT (G)	CARBS (G)	FIBER (G)	PROTEIN (G)
Hazelnut Coffee Pancakes	174	8	16	5	8
Strawberry Shortcake Waffles	590	42	45	8	11
Cherry Almond Streusel Muffins	221	15	19	3	5
Honey Nut Crunch	253	19	18	3	5
Gingerbread Muffins	164	10	15	2	3
Biscuits	290	37	16	2	2
Chunky Monkey Muffins	243	17	21	4	5
Dairy-Free Strawberry Yogurt	300	30	9	0	2
Cowboy Hashbrown Skillet	624	42	37	6	27
Sausage & Eggs To Go	249	18	1	0	18
Western Omelette To Go	82	5	.5	0	8
Caprese Baked Eggs	139	9	5	1	9
Smoked Salmon Hash	299	6	25	3	36
Bacon Ten Ways	130	10	0	0	9
Coconut Shrimp Cakes	234	6	4	2	30
Crawfish Étouffée	173	6	7	1	20
Seafood Pot Pie with Cheddar Crumble Biscuit	357	18	12	1	35
Pastrami Salmon	236	9	4	0	33
Shrimp Pad Thai	189	11	11	1	38
Gyro Taco Salad & Tzatziki Guacamole	476	40	3	2	26
Spanakopita Soup	378	28	5	4	24
Moo Shu Cabbage Cups	392	22	3	1	43
Best-Ever Pulled Pork	389	22	0	0	43
Cuban Burger	435	21	27	5	45
Spaghetti Squash Carbonara	359	24	15	3	22
Balsamic Onion & Arugula Pizza	188	10	18	1	6
Butternut Squash Lasagna	500	37	22	4	19
Loaded Fauxtato Soup	198	14	12	6	9
Chorizo Stuffed Pork Chop	310	18	7	1	28
Bacon Lattice & Tomato Sandwich	363	31	2	1	19
Chicken Enchilada Empanadas	470	23	53	0	13
Sweet & Sour Split Roast Chicken	225	8	8	0	30
Crispy Chicken Fingers	257	13	14	0	19

	CALORIES	FAT (G)	CARBS (G)	FIBER (G)	PROTEIN (G)
Thai Chili Chicken Meatballs	284	12	21	0	17
Hot & Sour Chicken Noodle Soup	412	10	34	0	47
Tikka Masala Chicken Wings	318	24	1	0	25
Curry Turkey Burgers & Mango Slaw	238	10	15	2	22
Buffalo Chicken Salad	213	19	4	0	16
Chili Pie	499	26	27	2	42
Italian Fajitas	262	16	4	1	25
Pumpkin Chili & Zesty Guacamole	365	24	13	5	24
Philly Stuffed Peppers	238	10	11	3	27
Chili Dog Chili	316	18	6	1	28
All-American Burger	454	23	25	2	34
Steak & Eggs Tartare	448	30	0	0	42
Sloppy Joe Meatballs	379	21	17	1	42
Chicago Dog Skewers	222	13	8	2	14
Swedish Meatloaf	426	30	9	1	27
Barbacoa Pot Roast	414	11	5	1	68
Antipasto Salad	353	19	10	4	28
Broccoli Salad	201	9	22	3	11
Caesar Egg Salad	345	29	2	0	38
Tabouli Salad	155	14	7	2	2
Tequila, Lime & Green Onion Slaw	189	14	10	6	3
Moroccan Carrot Salad	137	10	11	2	1
Roasted Squash & Beet Salad	163	9	22	4	3
Mediterranean Pasta Salad	136	14	3	1	1
Chimichurri Smashed Plantains	153	0	37	3	1
Sweet Potato Crisp	376	36	36	4	4
Coconut Curry Chowder	382	39	8	0	3
Mustard Roasted Asparagus	92	4	9	4	5
Baba Ganoush Gratin	260	16	10	6	7
Curried Creamed Spinach	87	5	4	2	4
Root Risotto	124	6	15	3	4
Ranch Potato Salad	261	18	22	3	3
Rosemary Parsnip Chips	147	7	20	1	1

	CALORIES	FAT (G)	CARBS (G)	FIBER (G)	PROTEIN (G)
Bloody Mary Pickled Tomatoes	39	0	8	1	1
Benedict Deviled Eggs	296	26	1	0	14
Guacamole & Bacon Pepper Poppers	257	21	16	7	5
Cheese Crackers	258	20	8	1	11
Beef Jerky	239	9	0	0	34
Barbecue Fauxtato Chips	219	17	13	5	1
Olive Oil Focaccia	132	15	19	2	2
Everything Crackers	277	16	29	0	4
B-Butter	171	17	5	1	6
Trail Mix Cups	85	5	10	0	1
Juicy Jigglers	38	0	8	0	2
Open-Faced Apple Pie	237	13	28	5	2
Blueberry Pastry Pies	246	13	30	6	2
Pecan Pie Squares	220	17	16	1	3
Mango Orange Cream Pops	96	4	16	1	0
Strawberry Lemonade Pudding	227	18	12	0	3
Cherry Limeade Sorbeta	98	1	24	2	1
Chocolate Almond Gelato	242	17	21	1	3
Caramelized Banana Milkshake	302	18	37	3	2
Thin Mints	133	9	13	1	3
Chocolate Coconut Scout Cookies	94	7	8	1	1
Chocolate Chip Cookies	139	8	17	1	1
Double Chocolate Espresso Cookies	146	8	8	1	3
Carrot Cake Cream Pies	345	31	20	1	4
Brownies	94	8	7	1	2
Dirty Blondies	76	6	6	3	1
Coconut Caramel Cupcakes	155	12	12	1	2
No-Bake Granola Bars	224	19	14	2	2
Almond Happiness Fudge	170	14	14	2	2
Devil's Food Snack Cake	173	14	13	1	2
Maple Banana Spice Cake	103	6	11	2	2
Bread	132	15	19	2	2
Pizza Crust	133	7	15	0	3

INDEX